this book belongs to

_____

_____

THANK YOU FOR YOUR PURCHASE

Welcome to "Floral Fantasy: Inverse Adult Coloring Book For Mindfulness and Stress Relief"! This unique coloring book offers a refreshing twist on traditional coloring books by providing intricate colorful designs with a floral theme to color in reverse.

What exactly does "Inverse coloring" mean? Instead of coloring inside the lines of a pre-drawn design, with a reverse coloring book, you start by drawing around the intricate designs. This creates a beautiful contrast between the colored background and the uncolored design, making it a satisfying and relaxing coloring experience.

The purpose of this coloring book is to provide a mindful and stress-relieving activity for anyone looking to unwind and get in touch with their creative side. Coloring has been shown to be a calming and meditative activity, helping to reduce stress and anxiety, increase focus and concentration, and promote relaxation.

Using this inverse coloring book is simple. Choose a design that speaks to you, and then start coloring the background around the intricate design. You can use colored pencils, markers, or any other medium of your choice. As you color, focus on the present moment and let go of any distractions or worries. Take your time and enjoy the process.

Once you've drawn the design from your imagination, take a deep breath and turn the page over to reveal the stunning completed design. The contrast between the colored background and the uncolored design will be a beautiful surprise, and you can further enhance the design with more colors if you wish.

We hope that "Floral Fantasy: Inverse Adult Coloring Book For Mindfulness and Stress Relief" brings you a sense of peace, relaxation, and joy as you explore your creativity and indulge in a moment of mindfulness. Happy coloring!

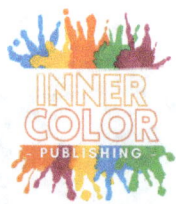

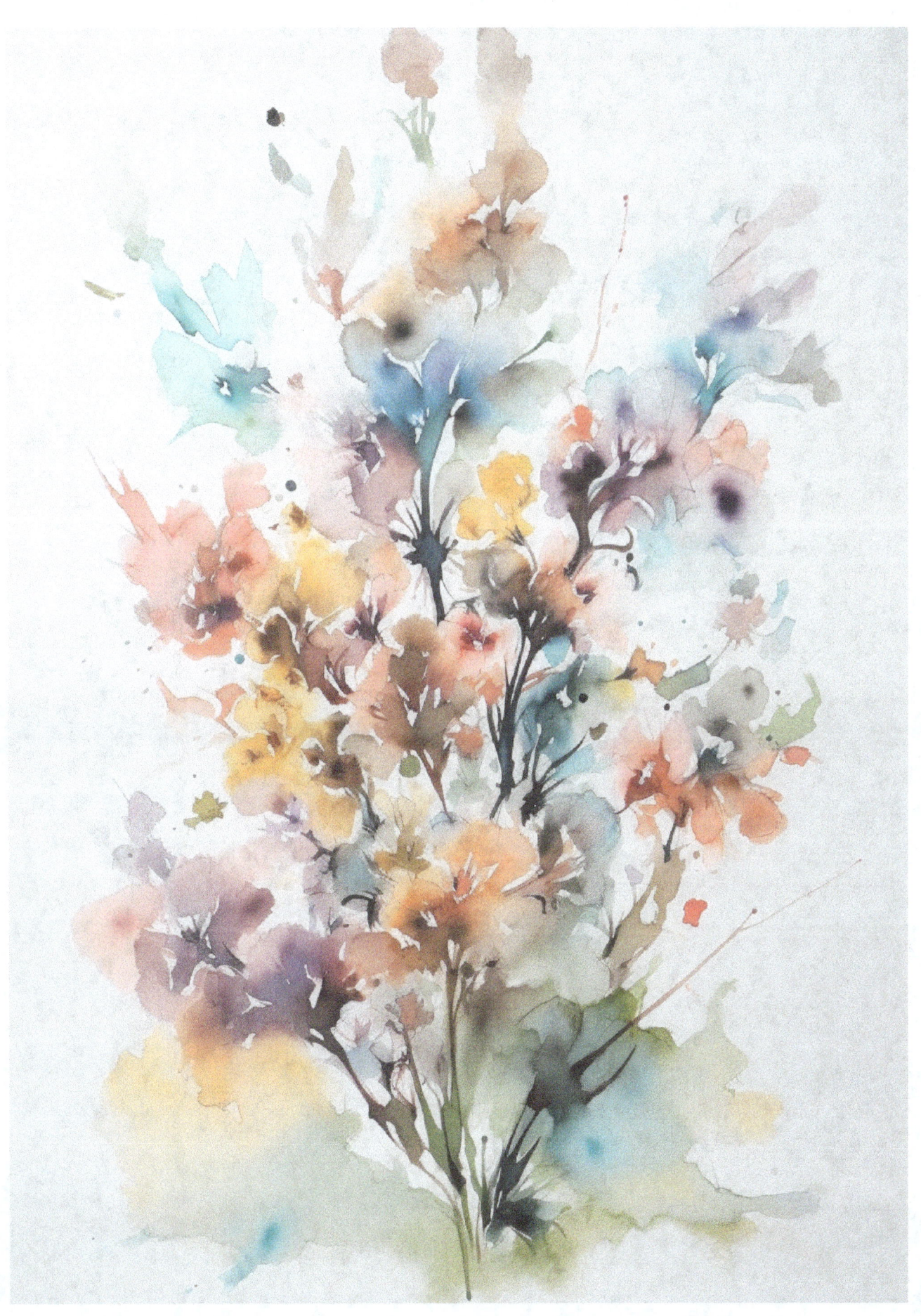

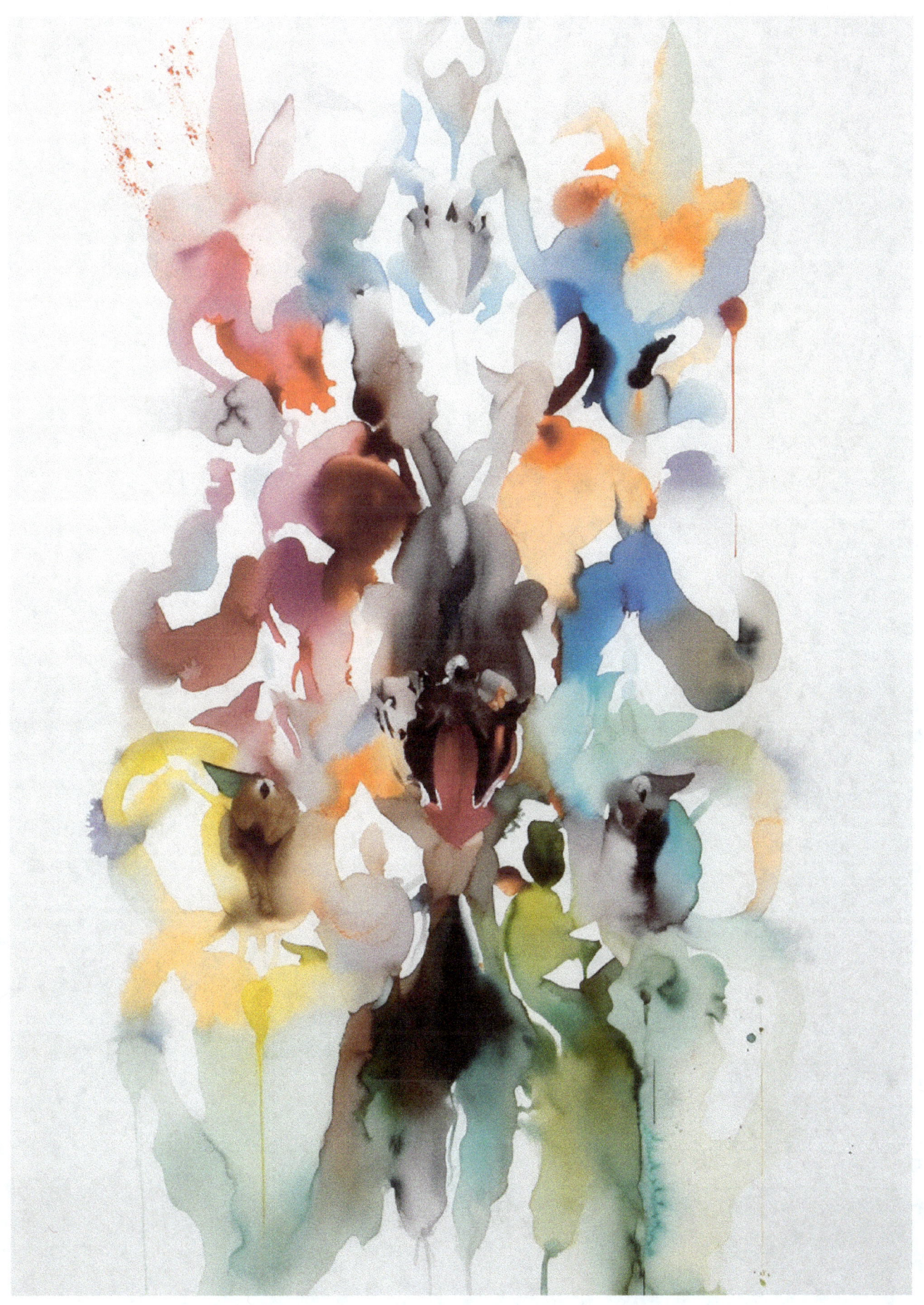

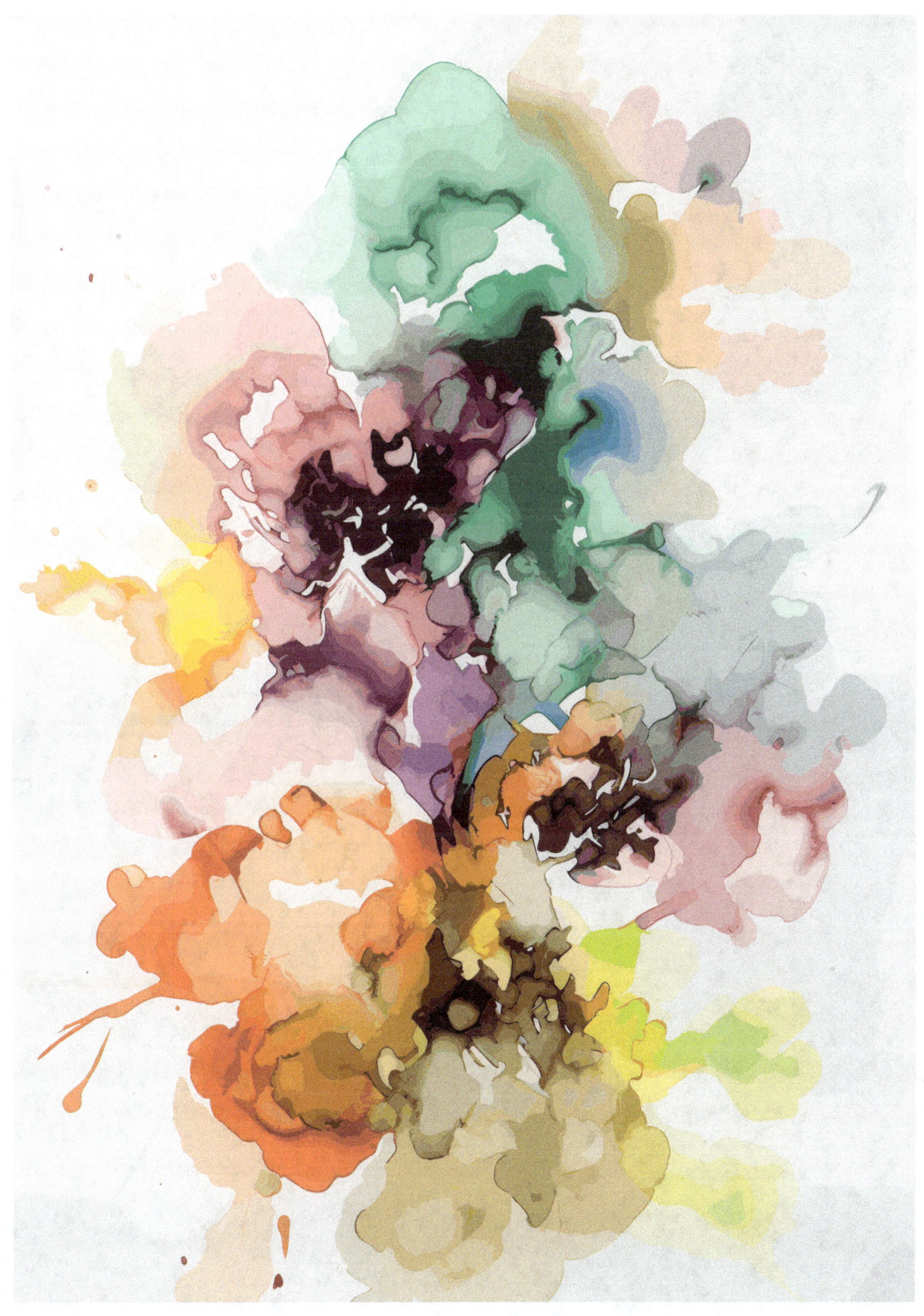

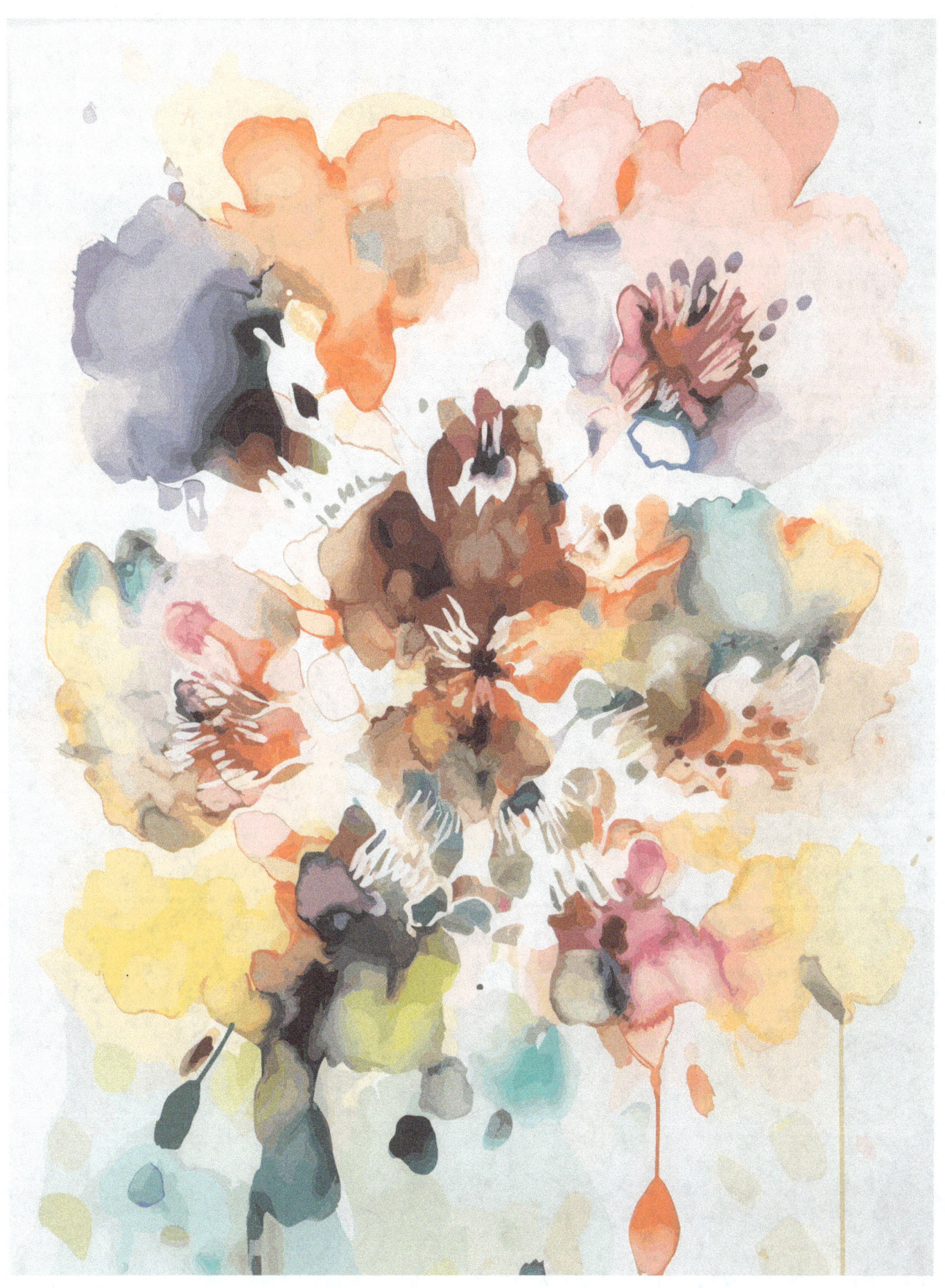

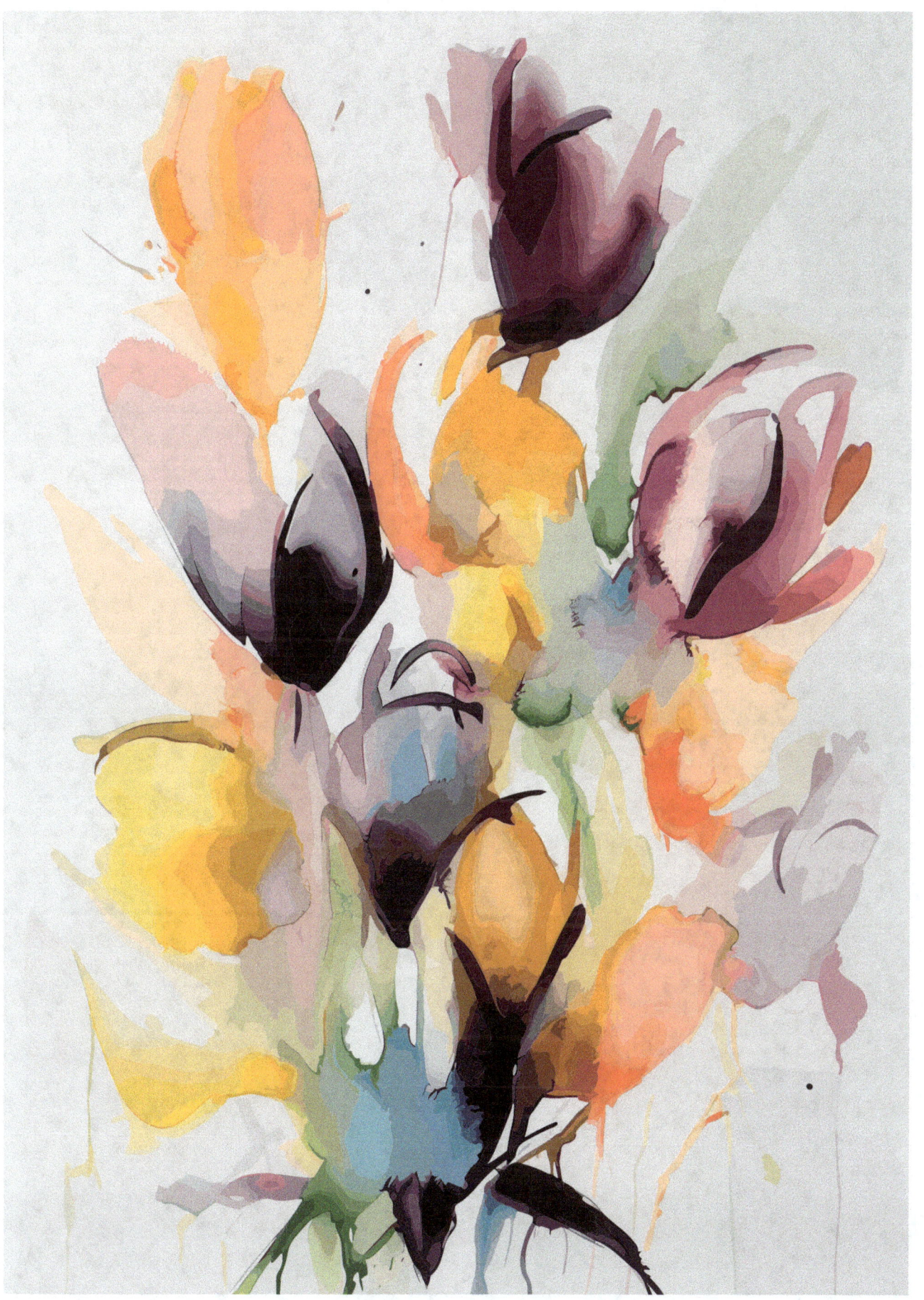

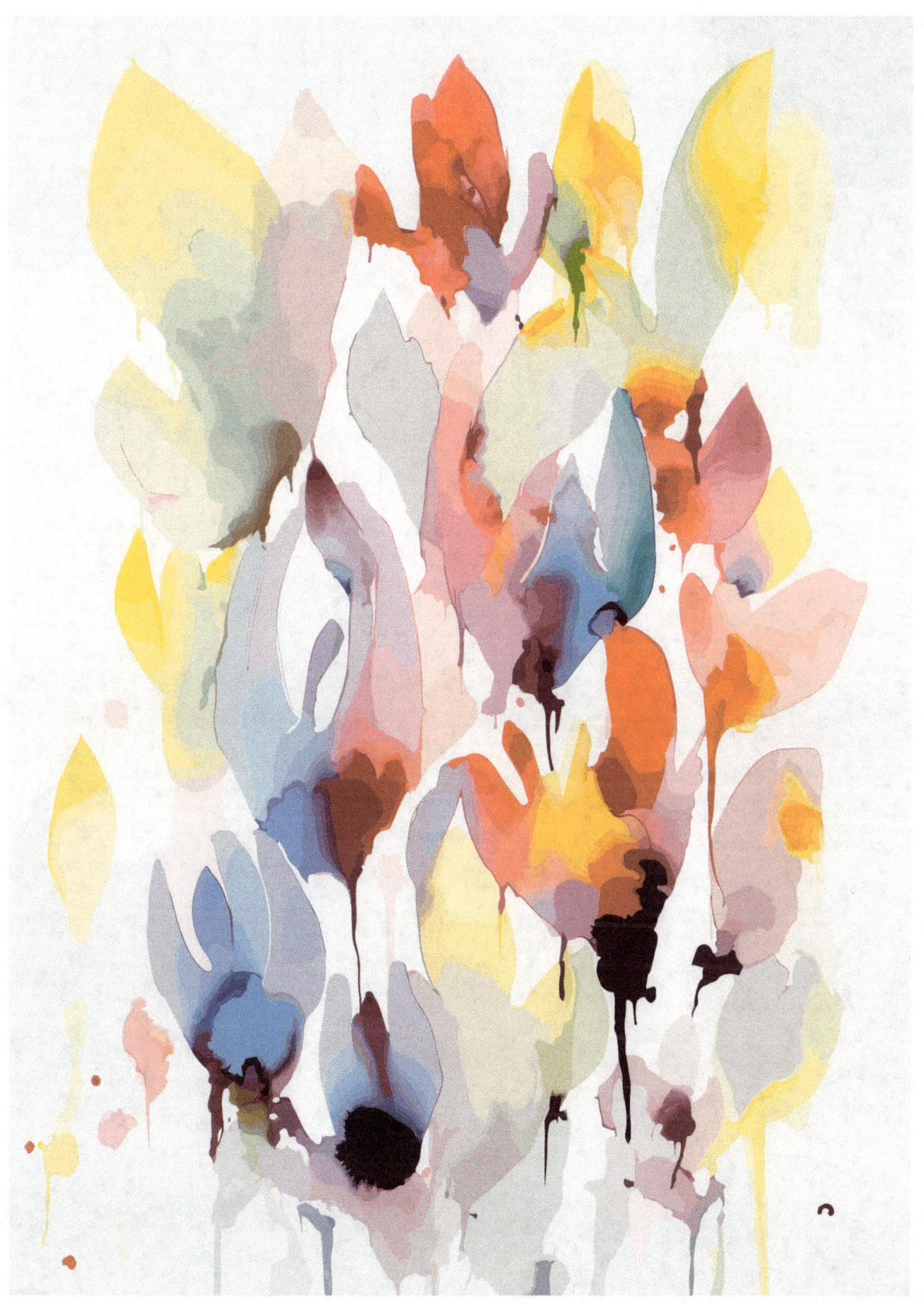

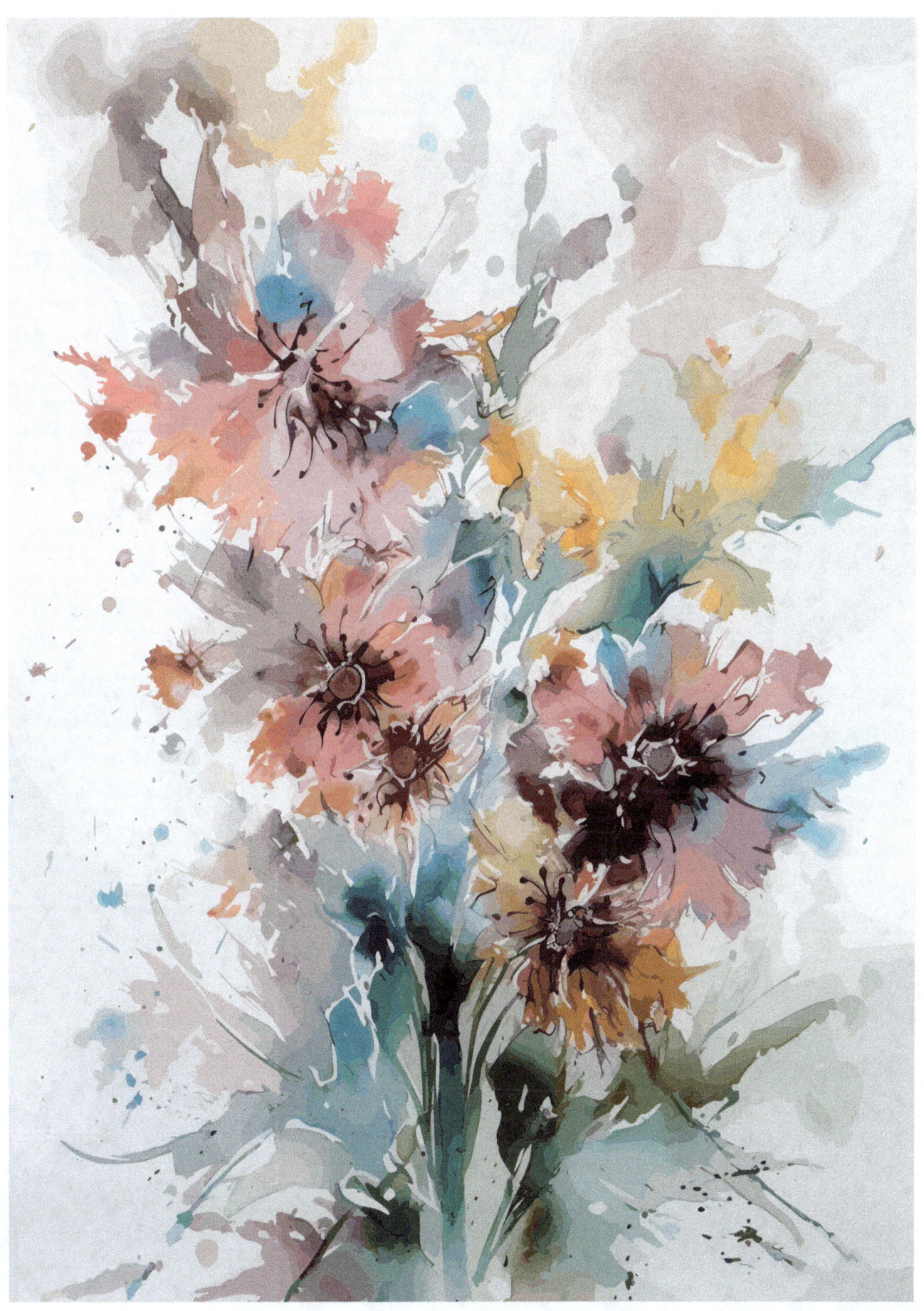

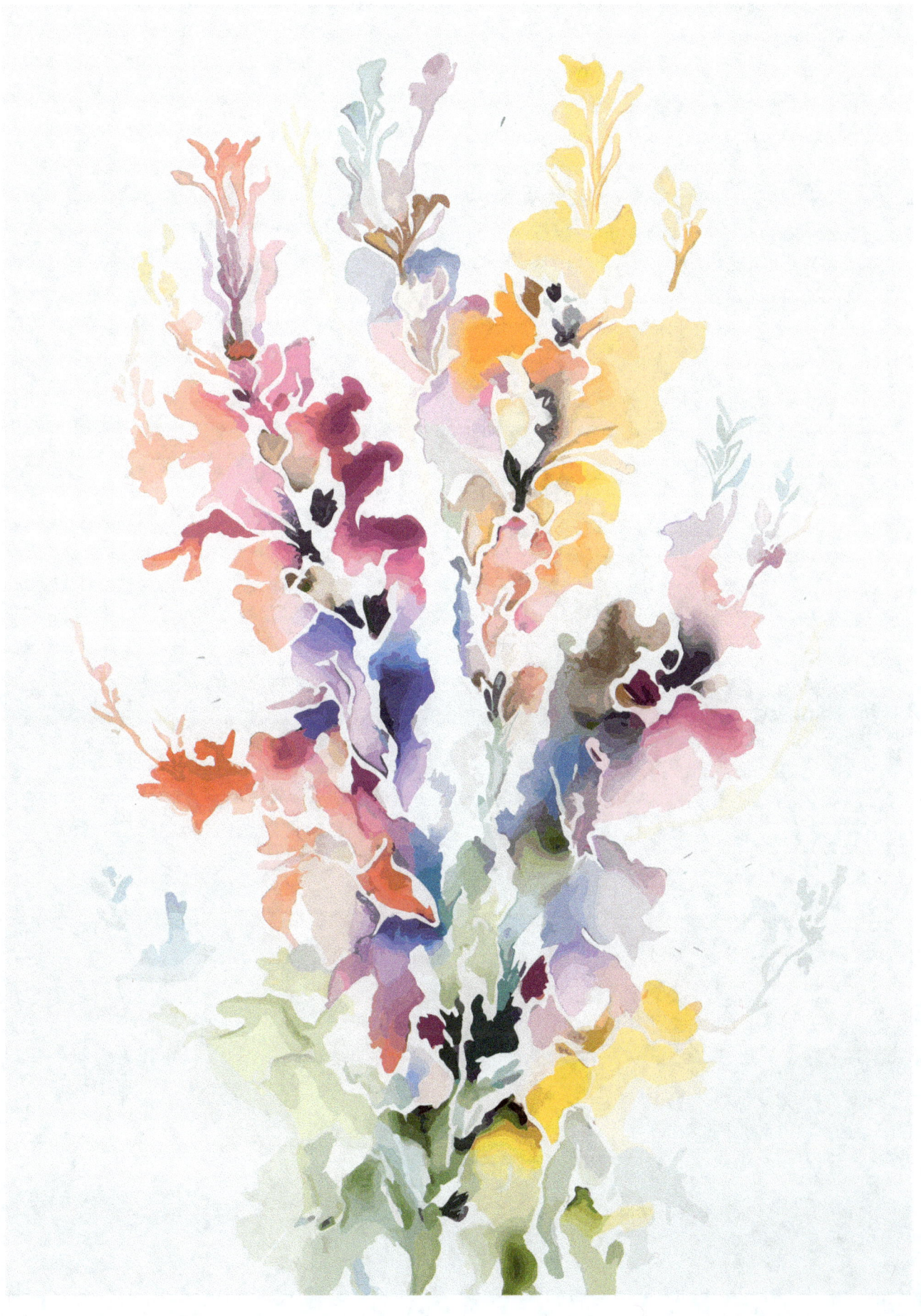

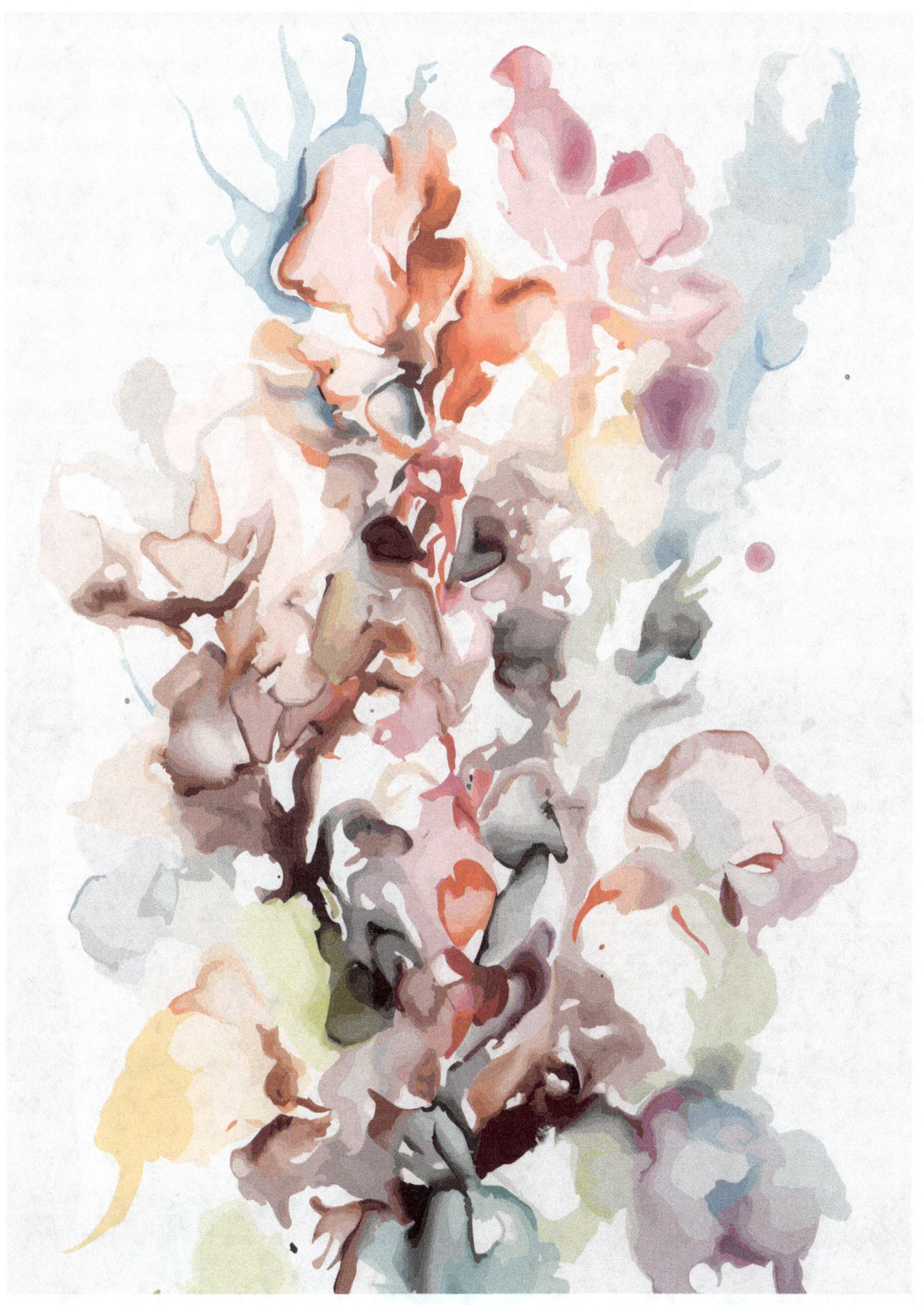

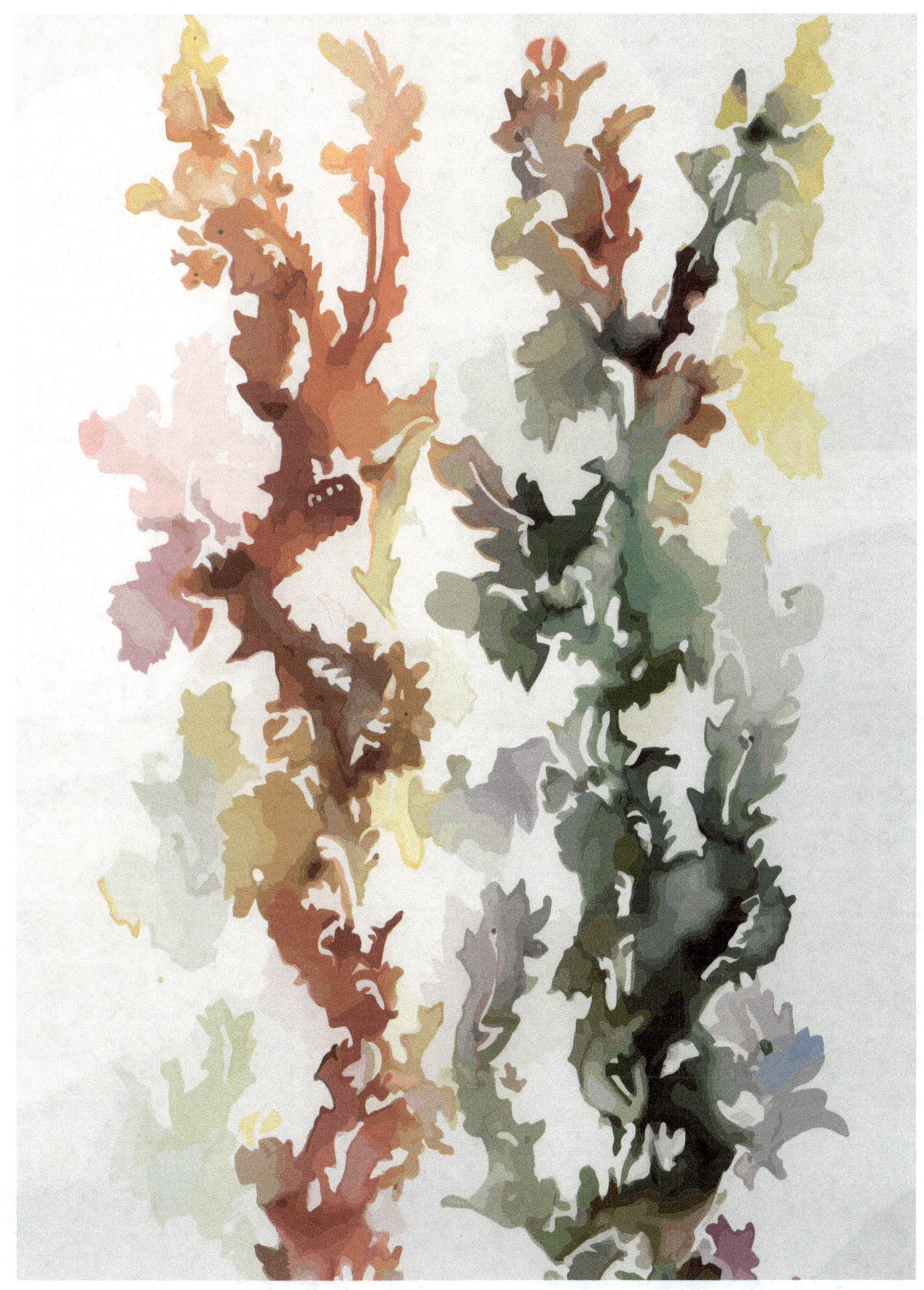

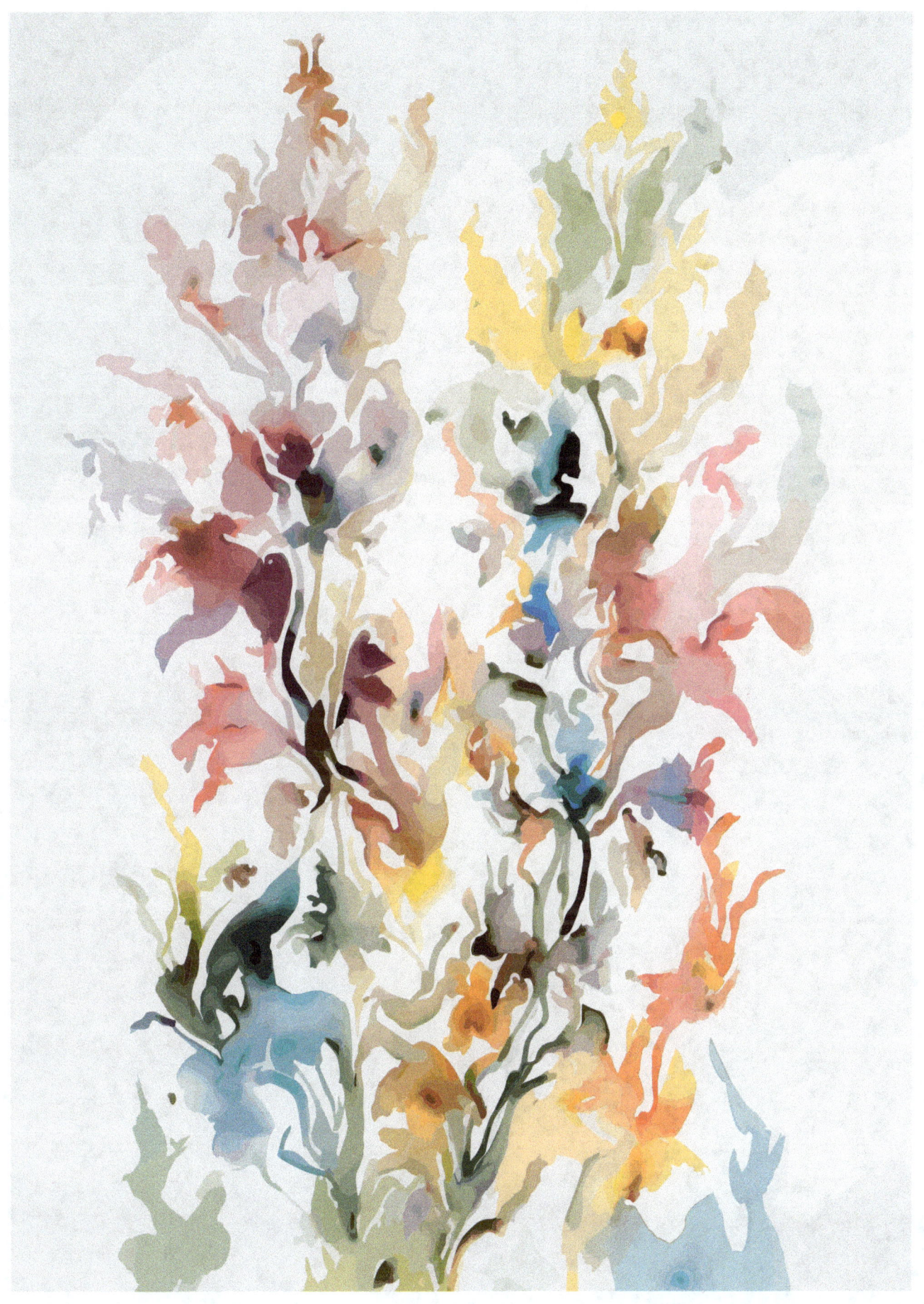

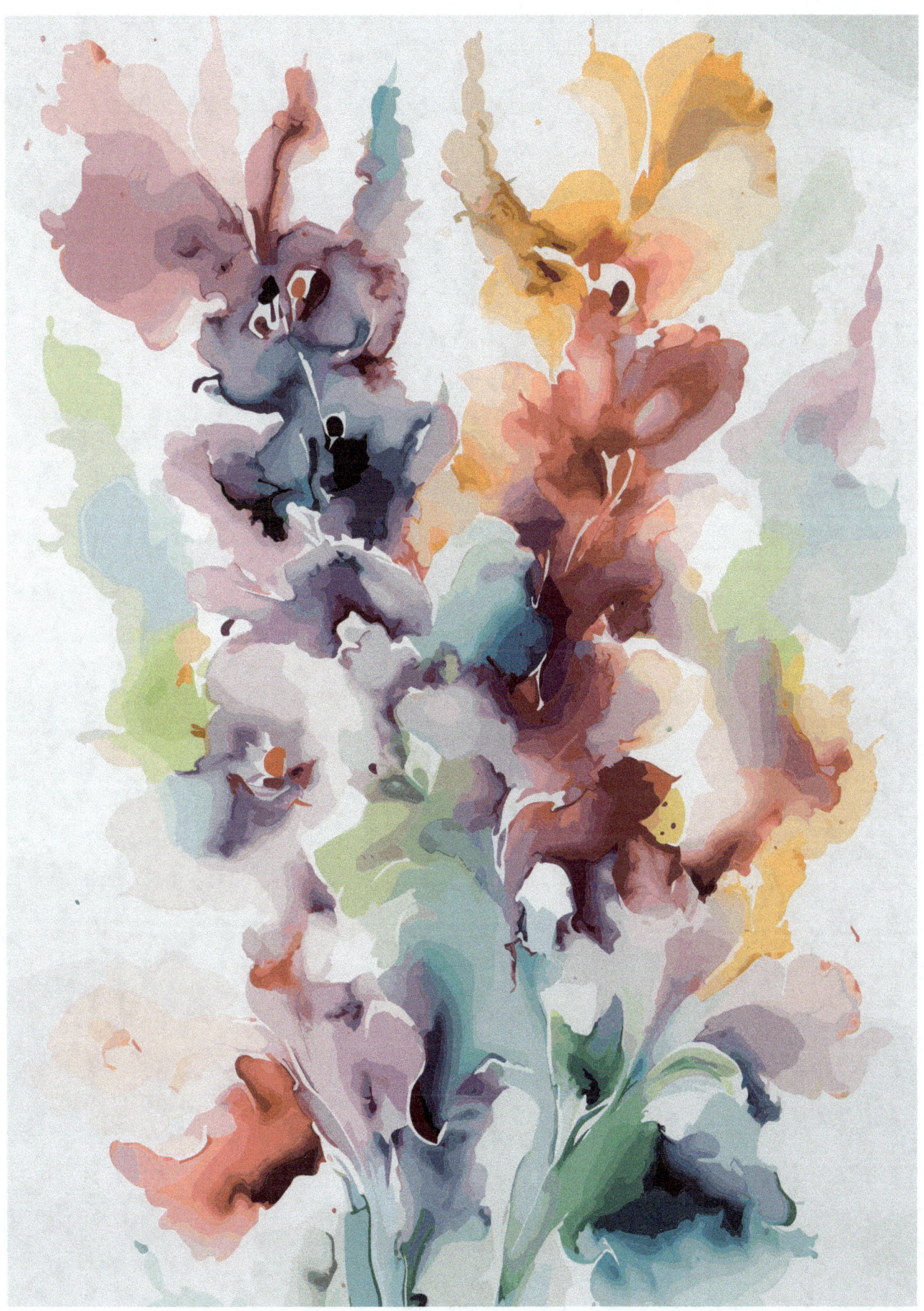

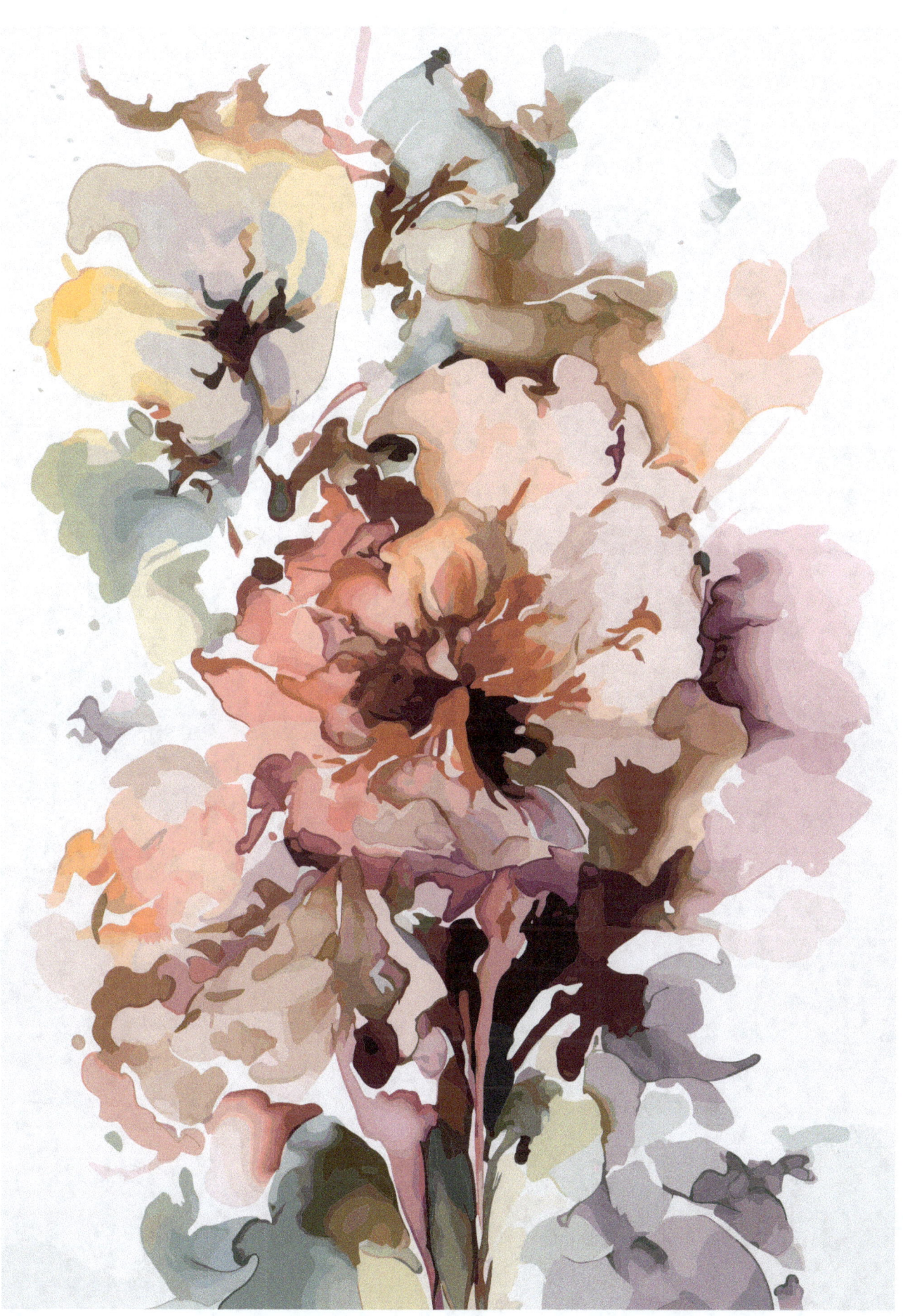

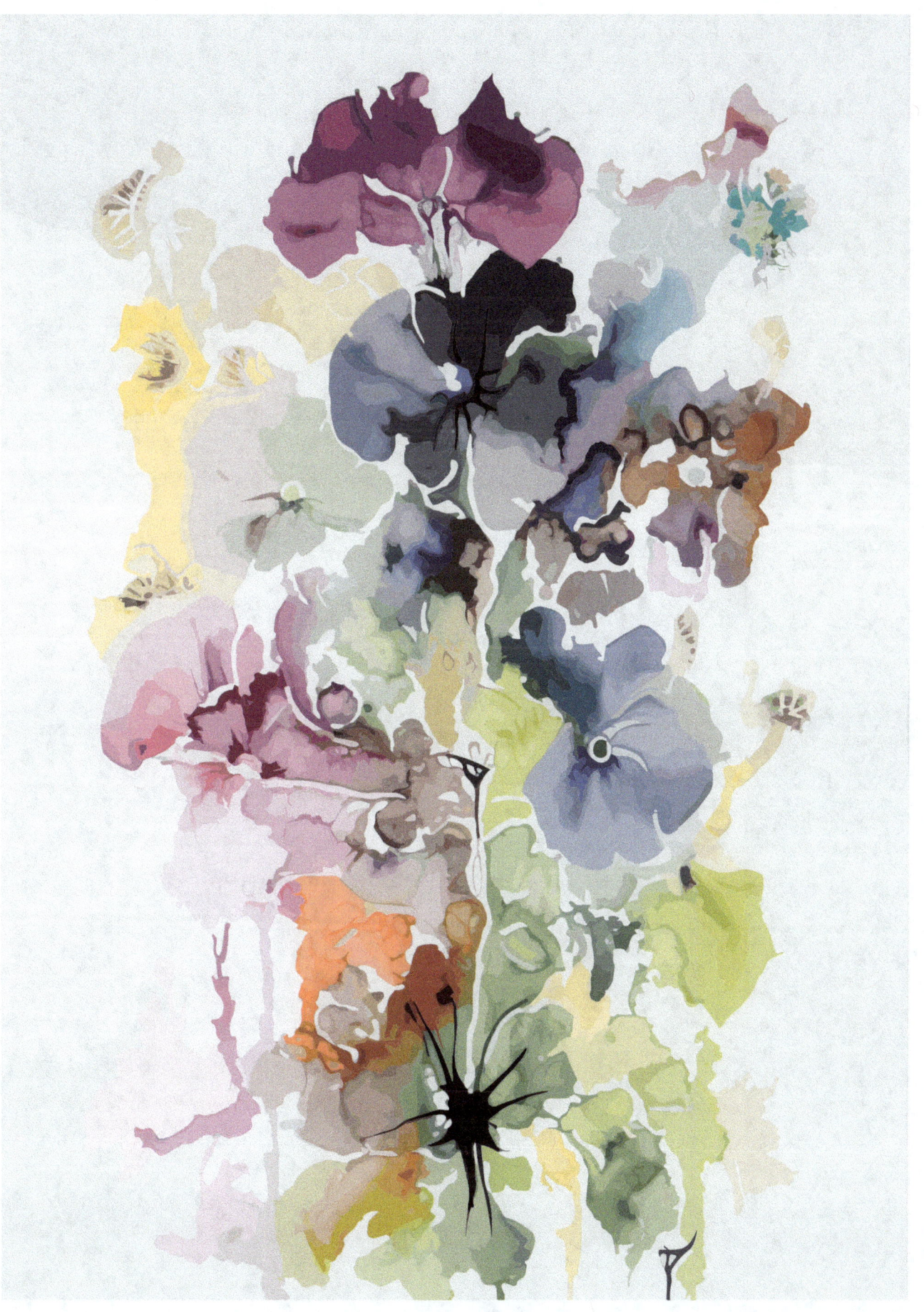

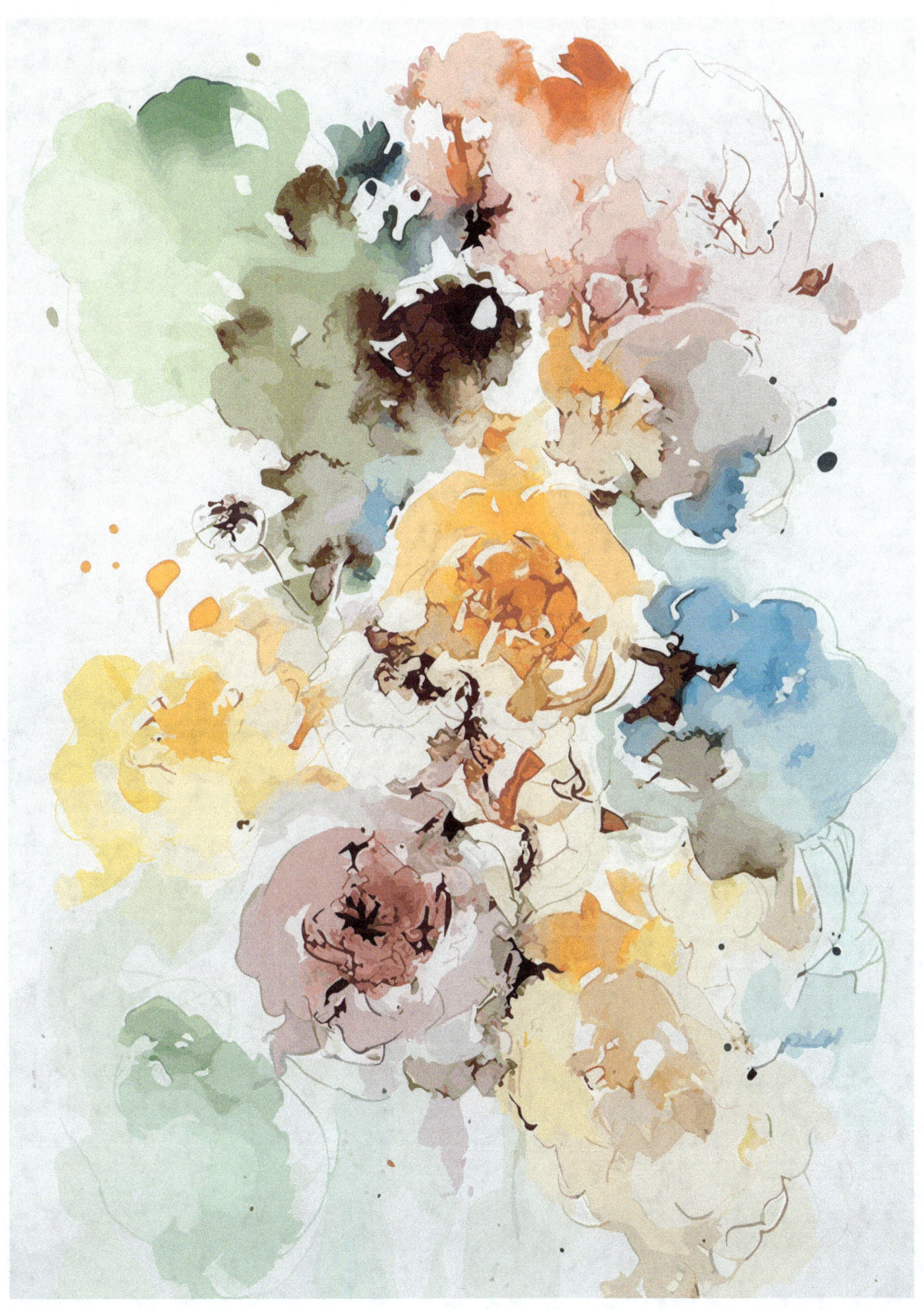

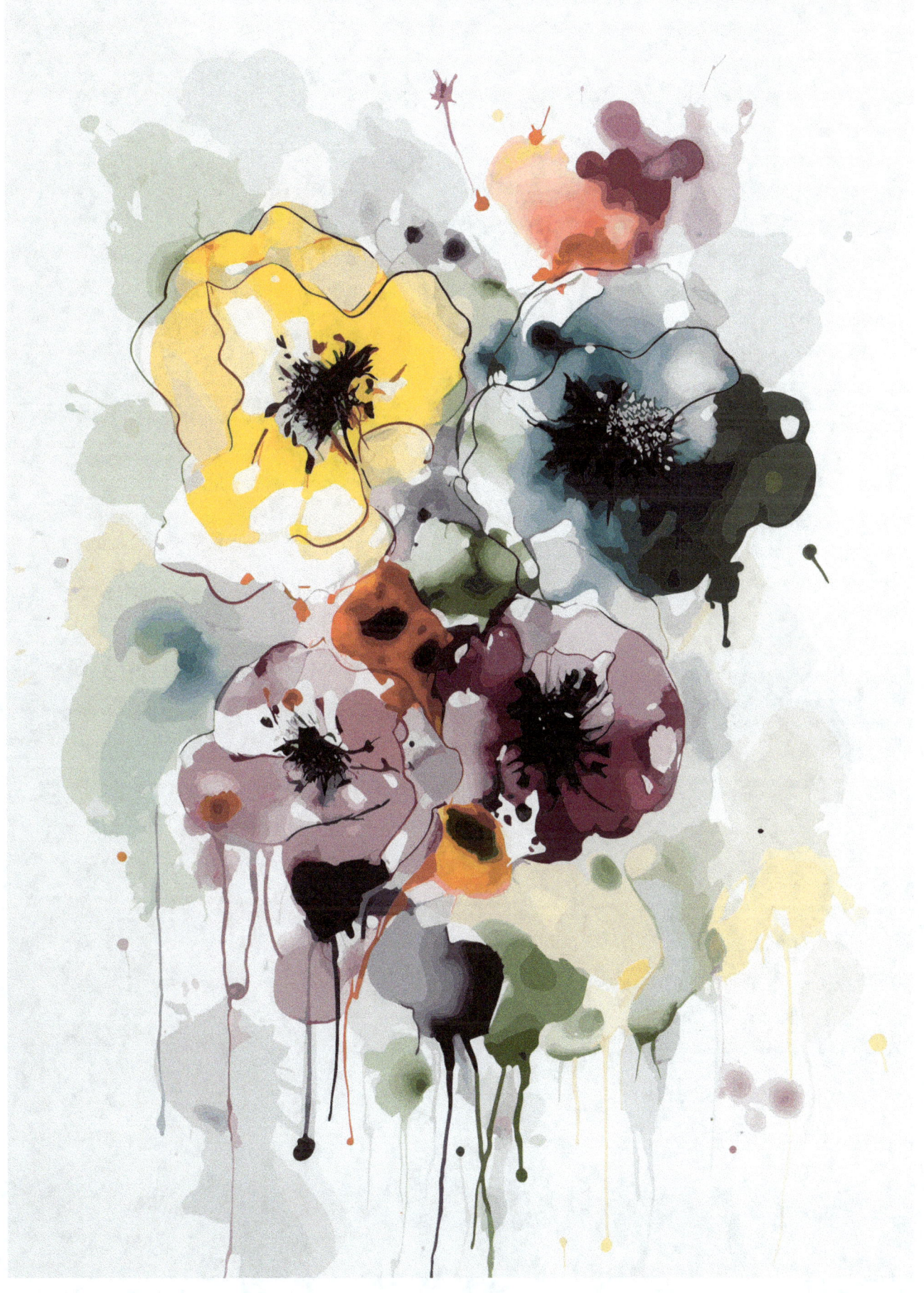

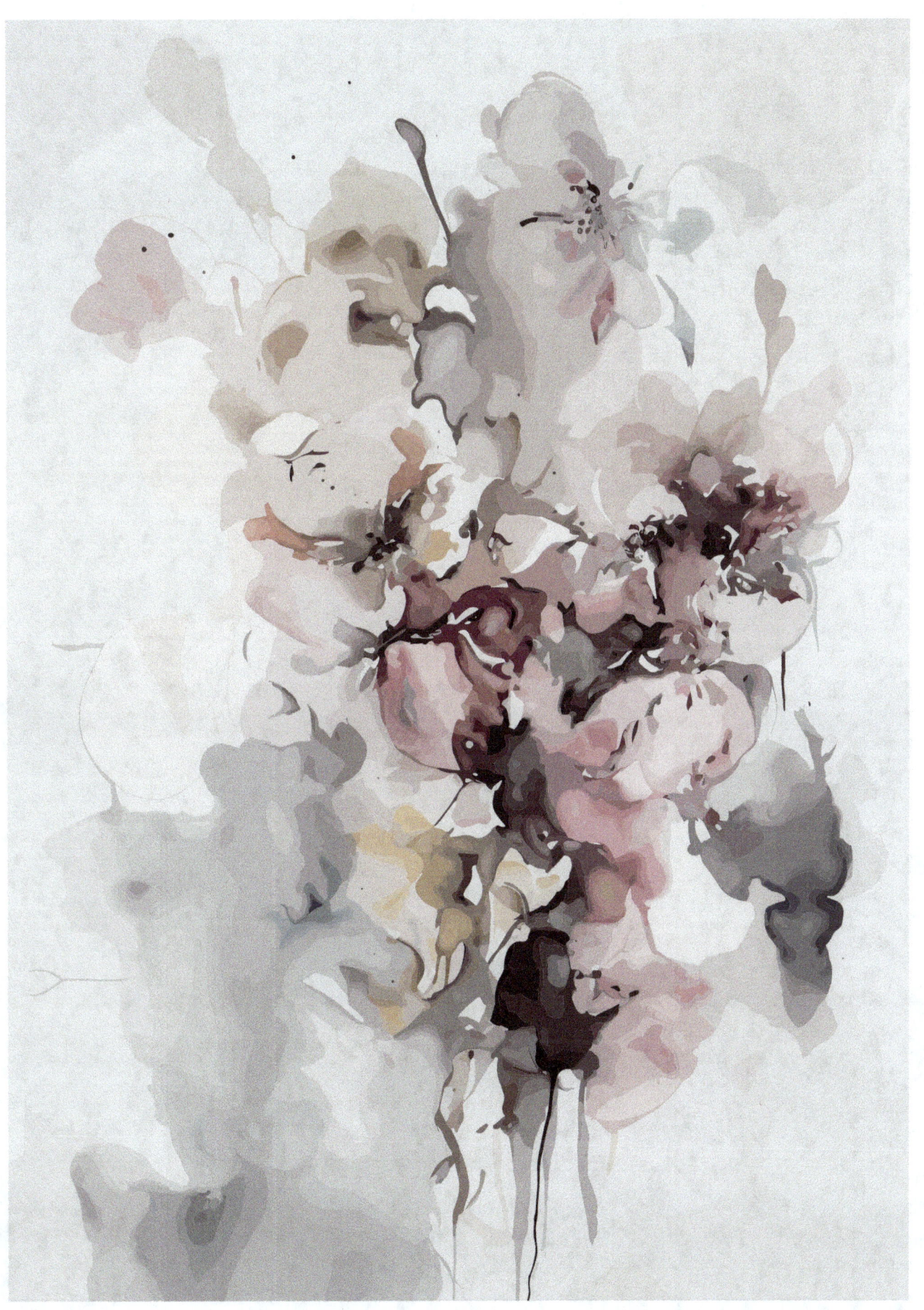

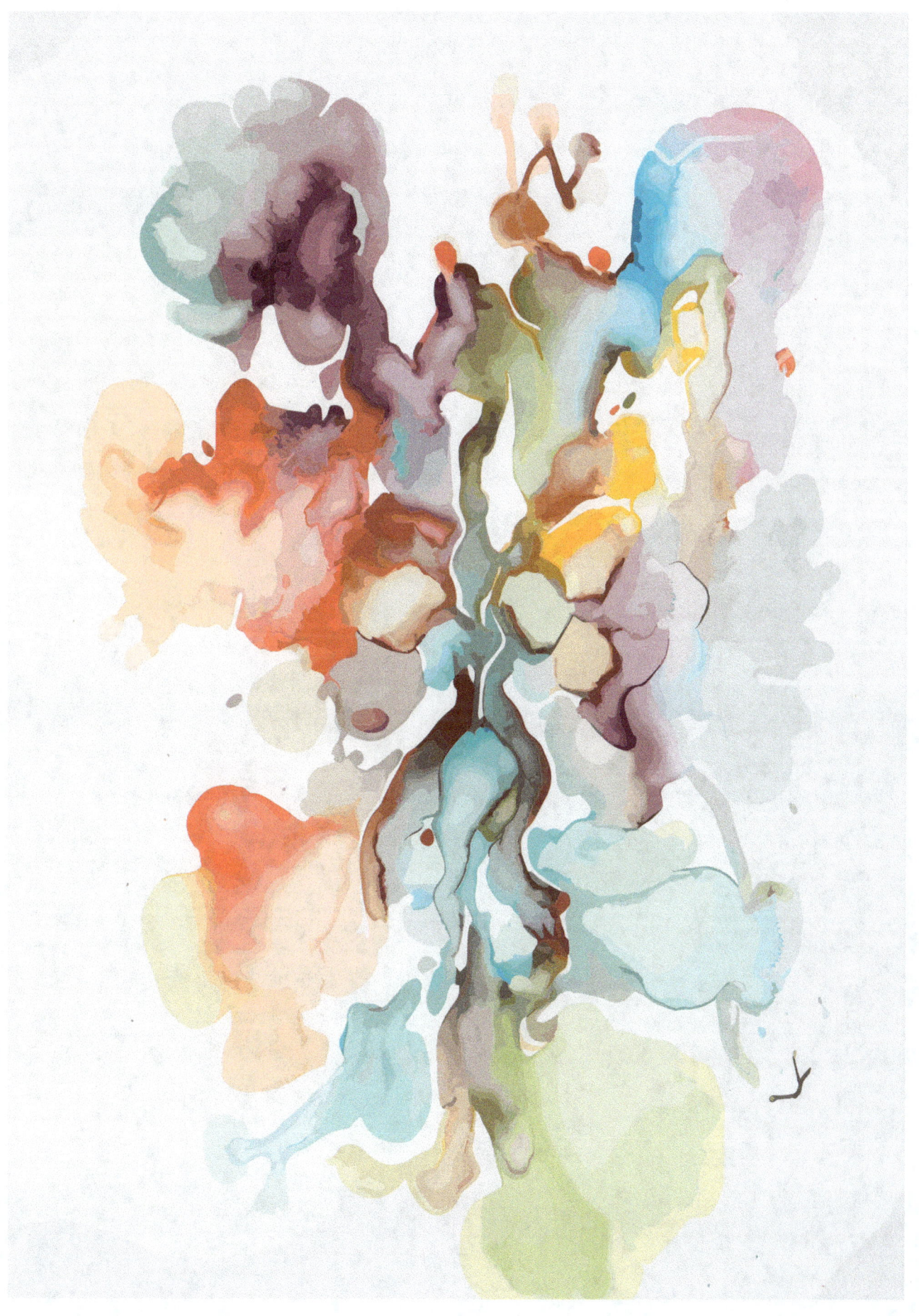

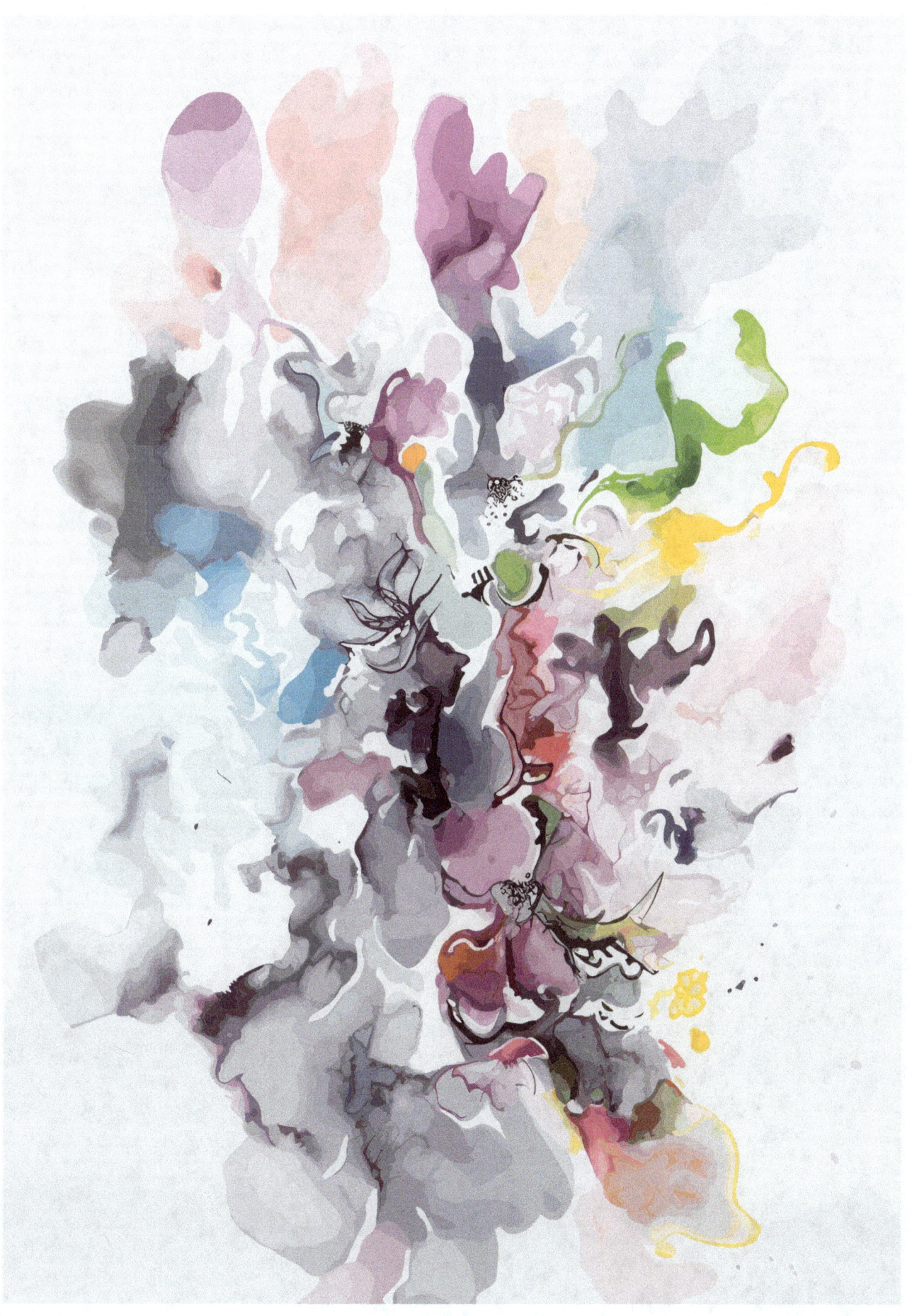

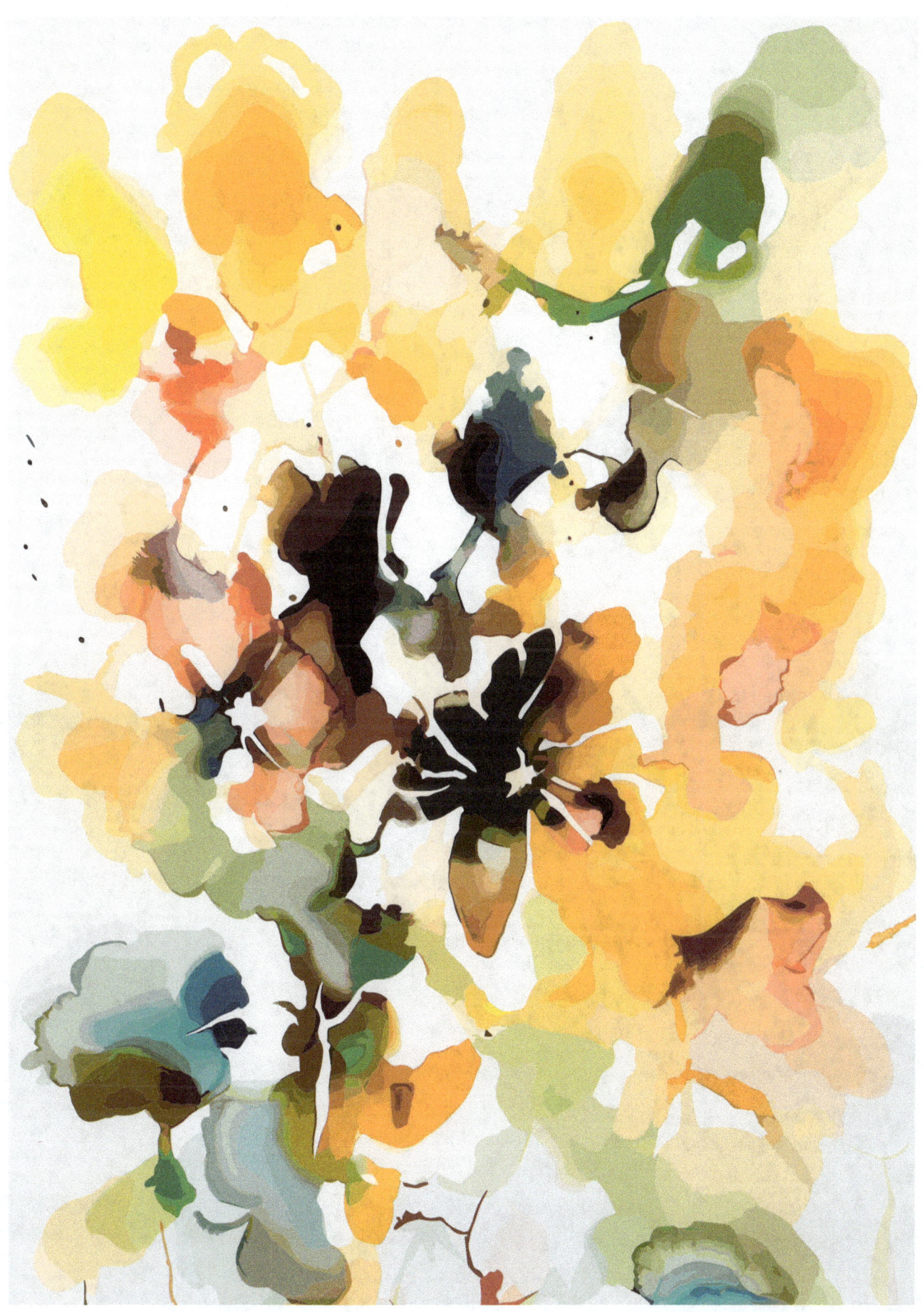

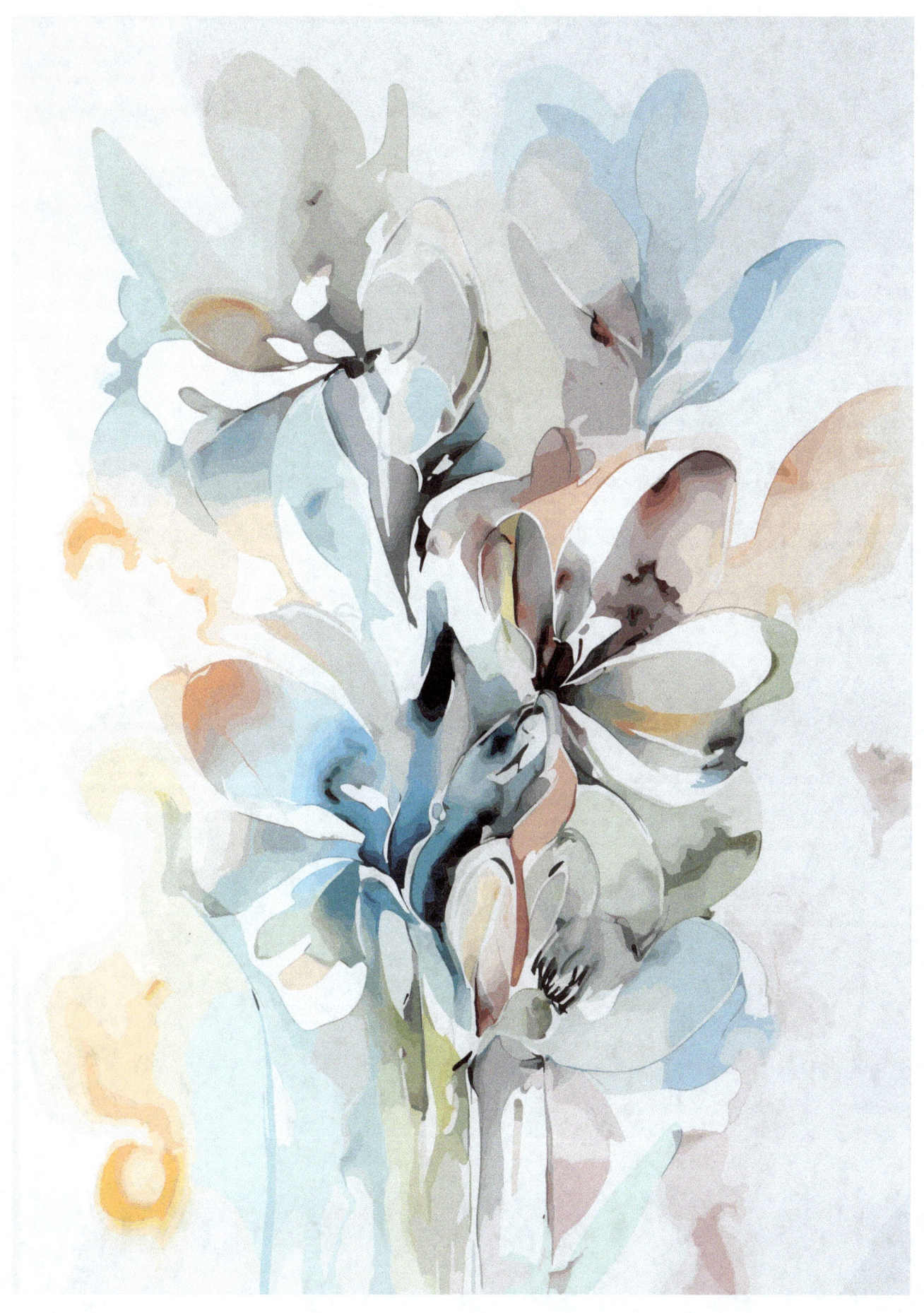

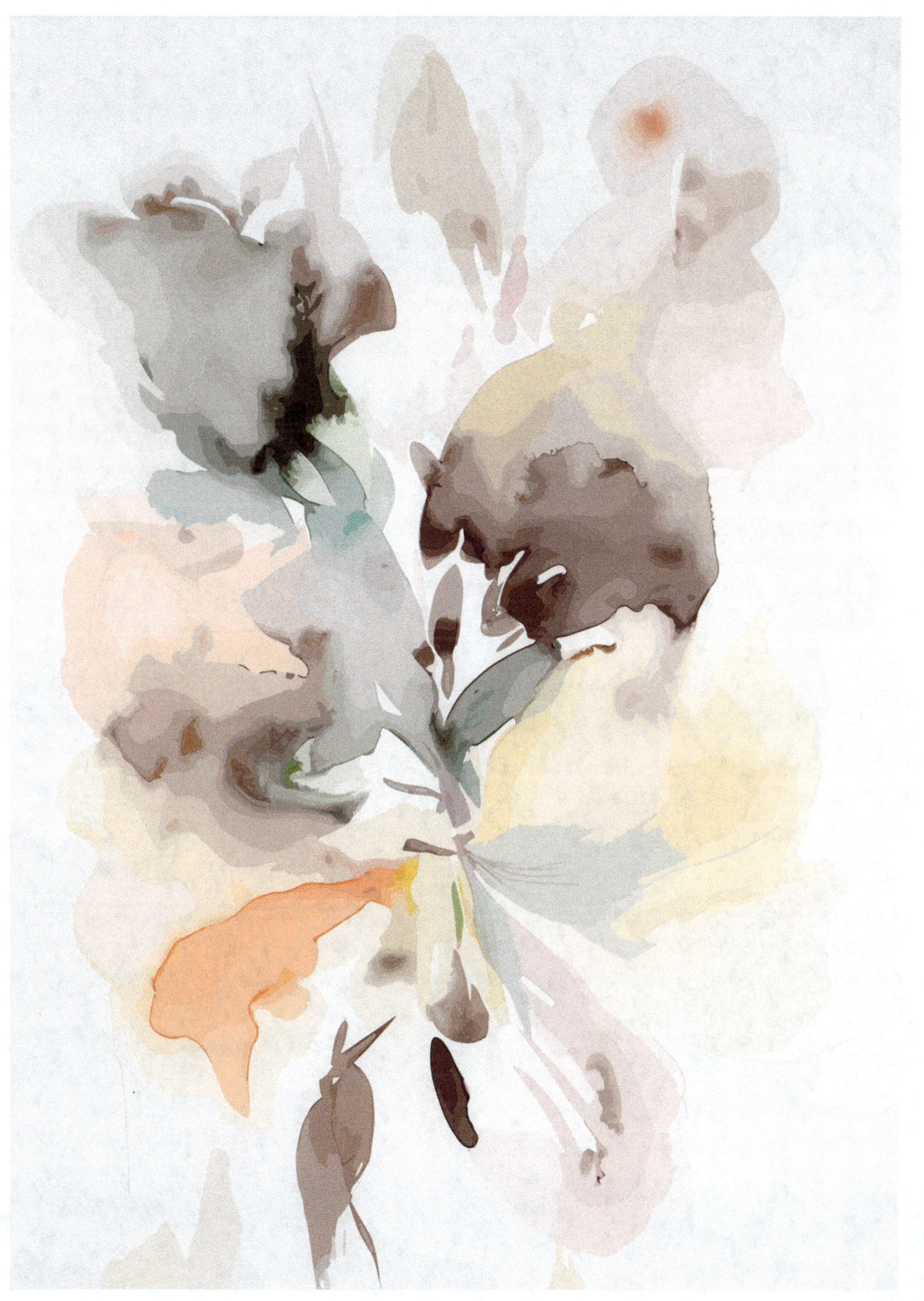

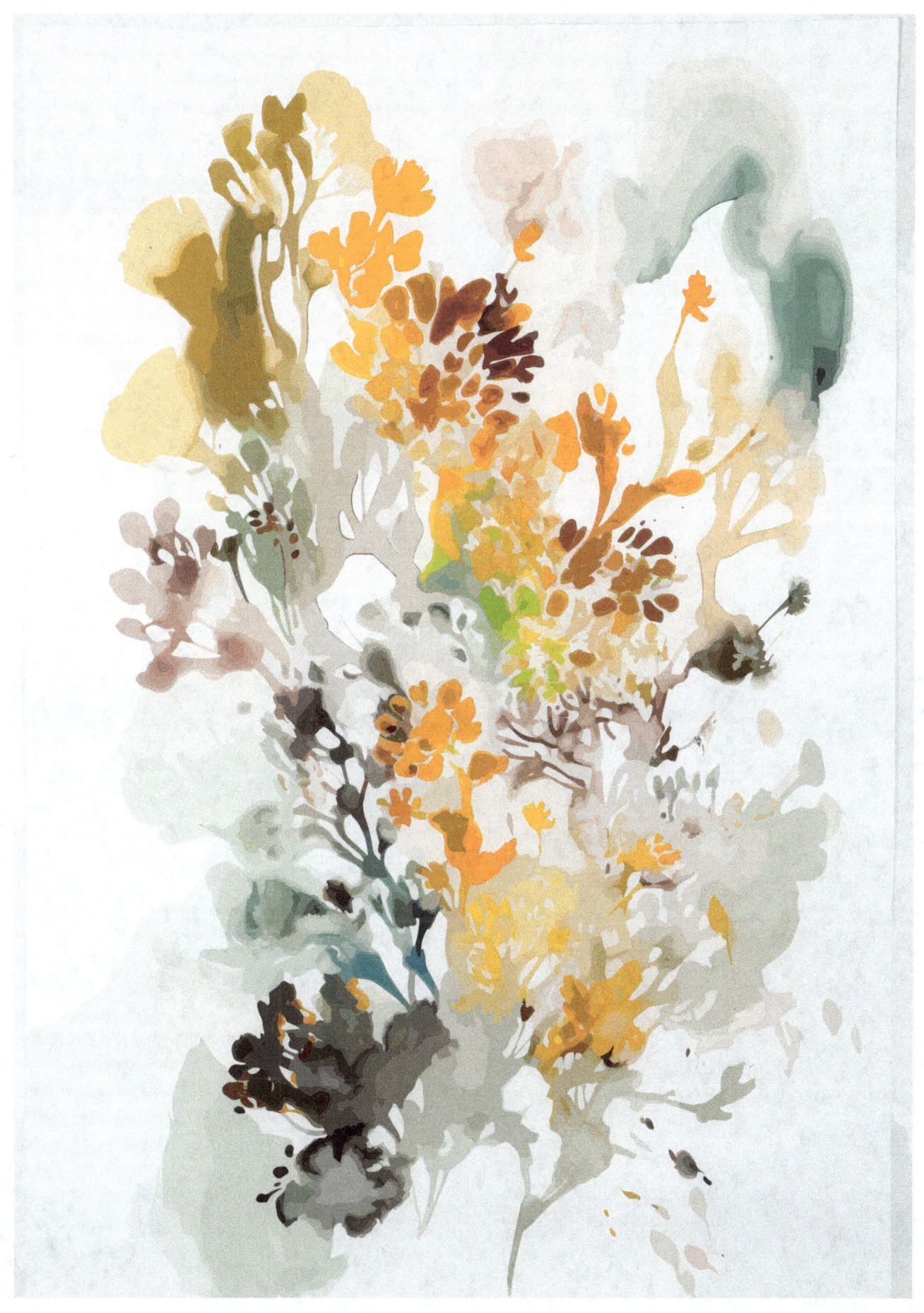

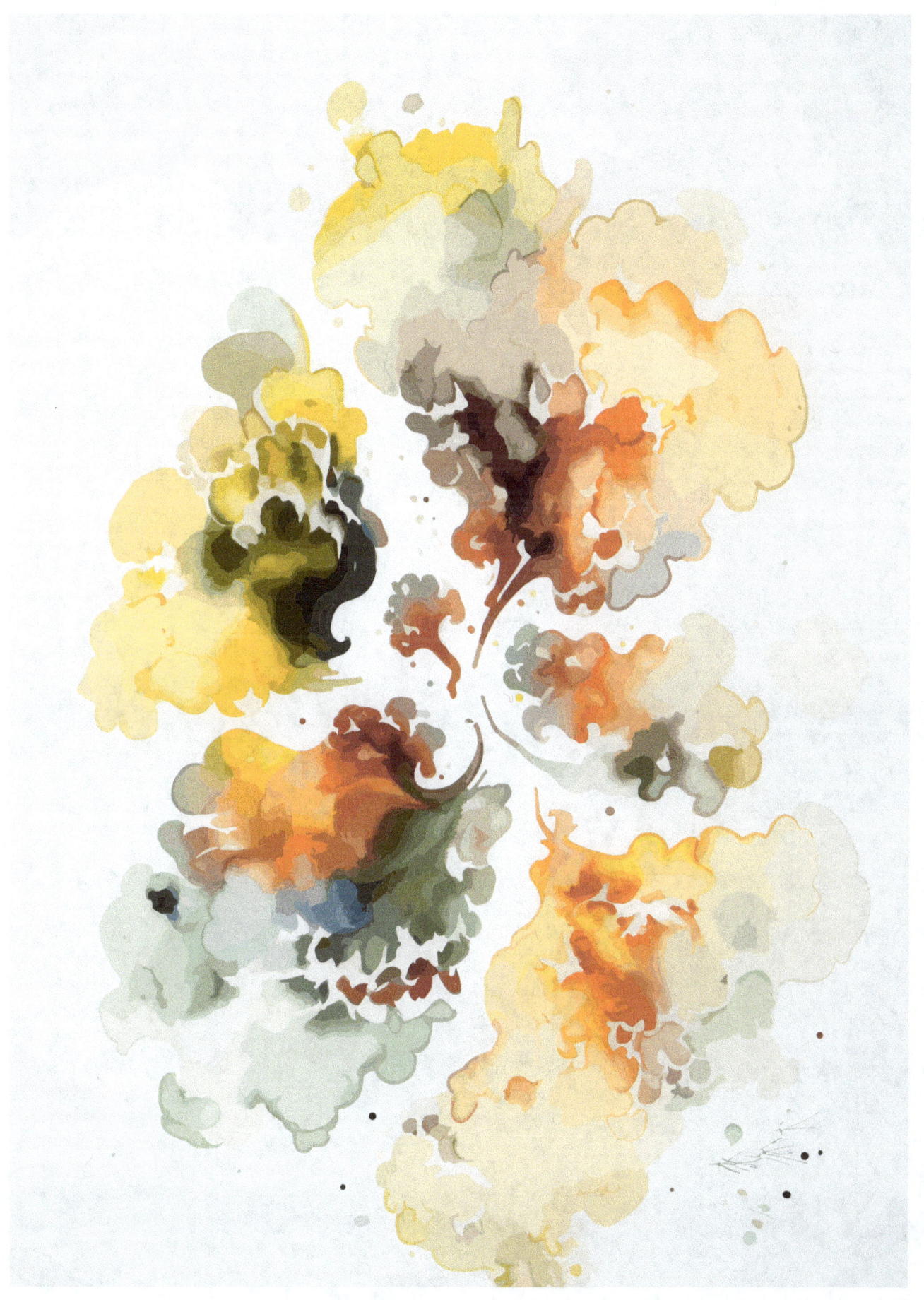

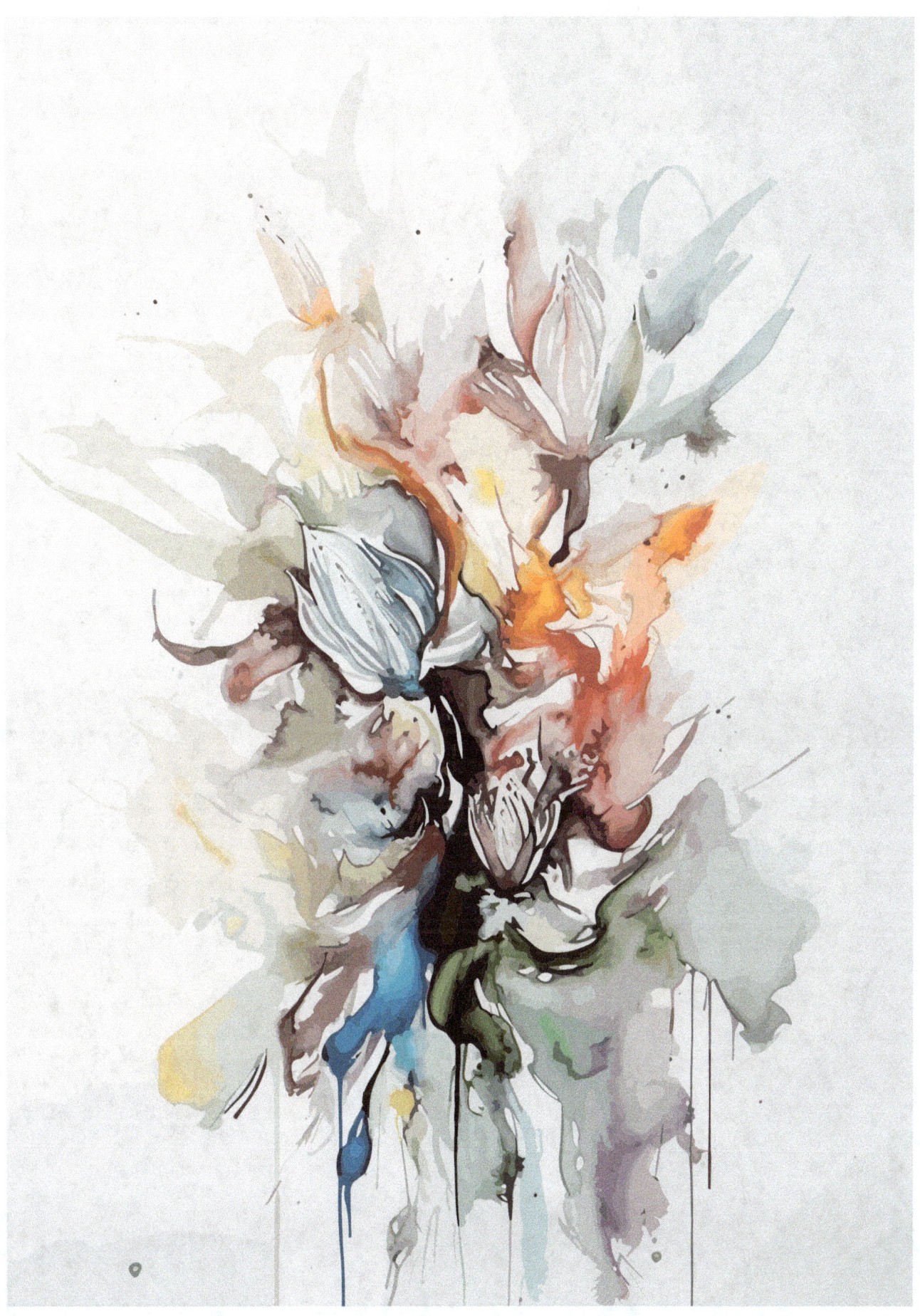

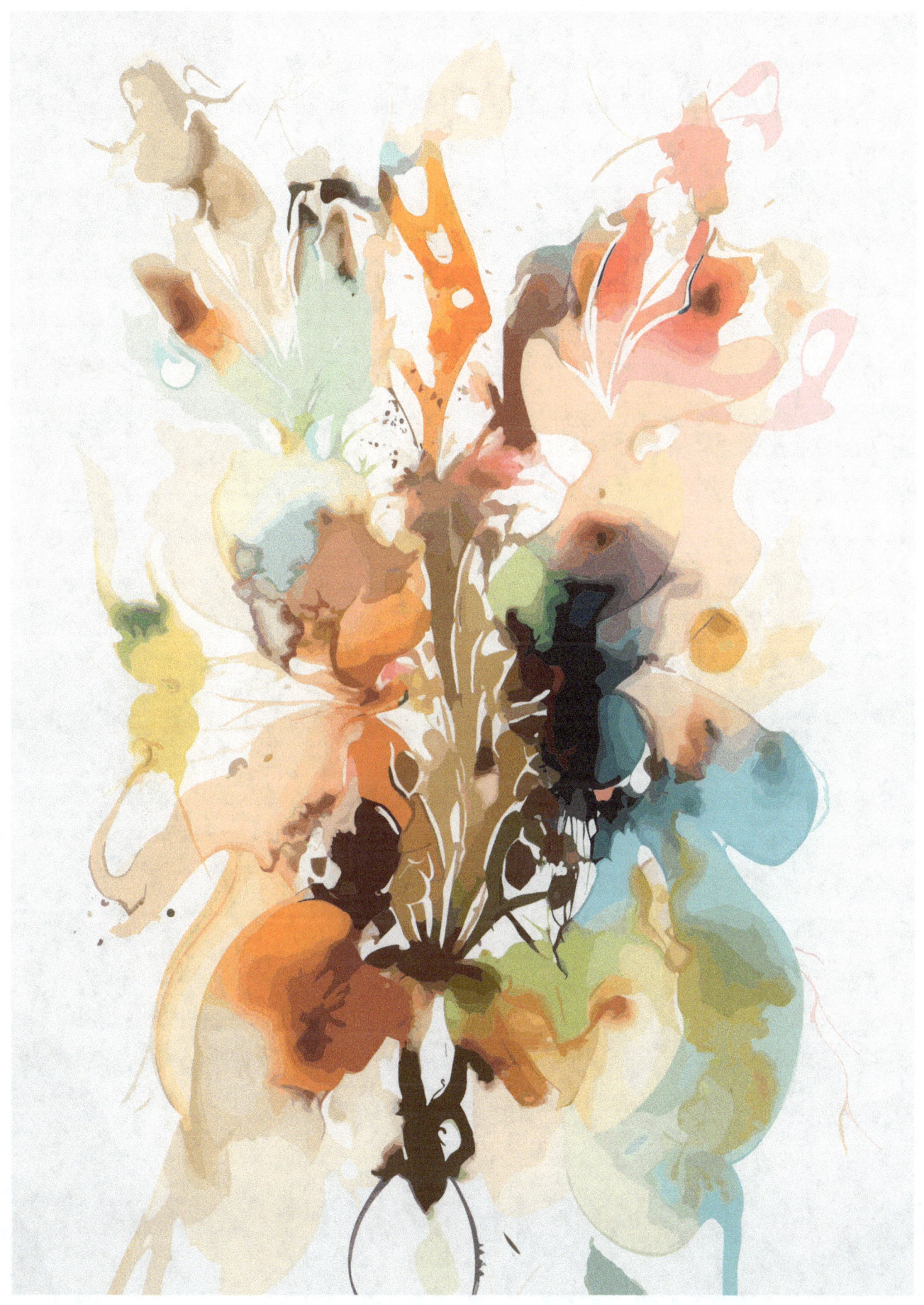

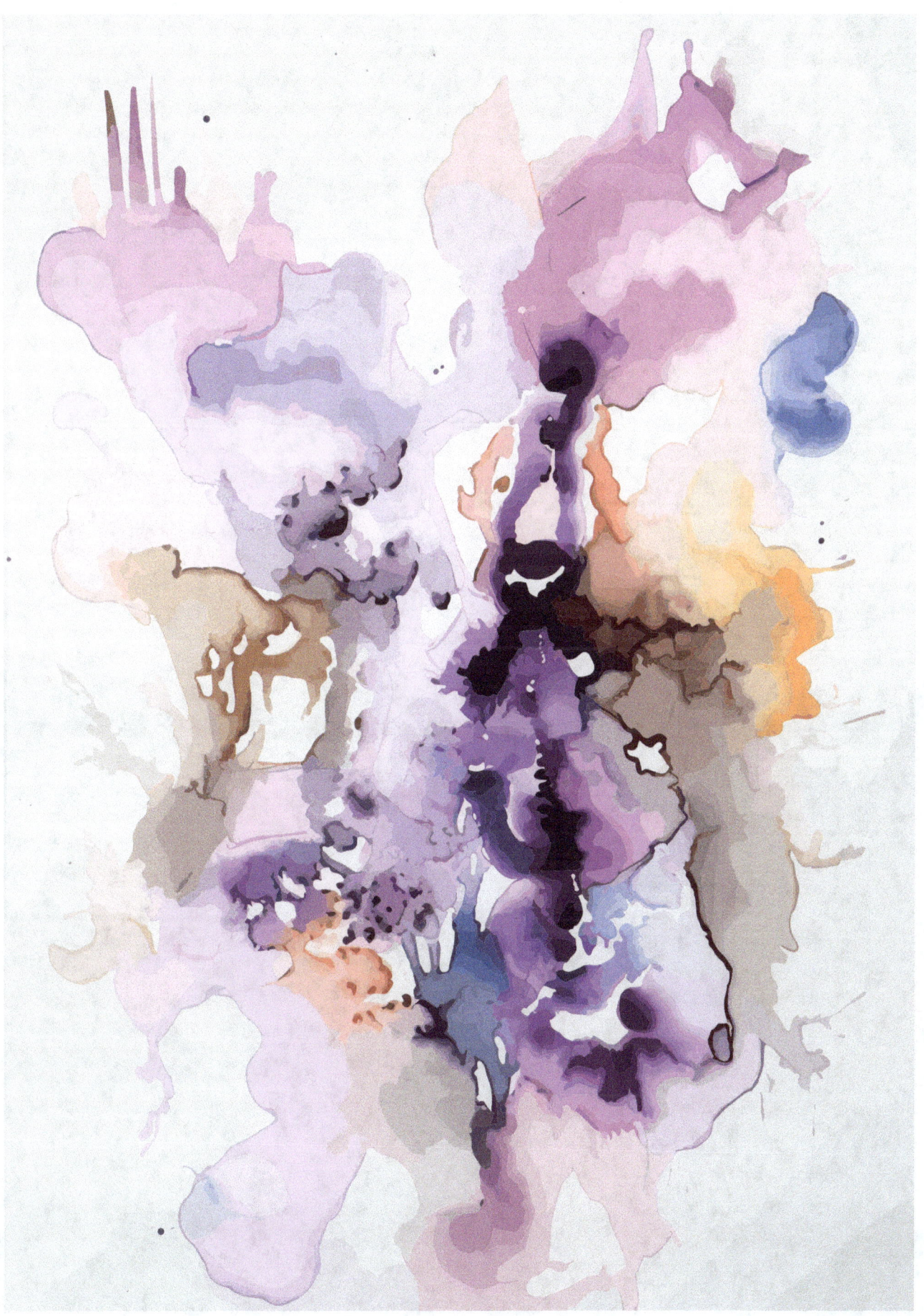

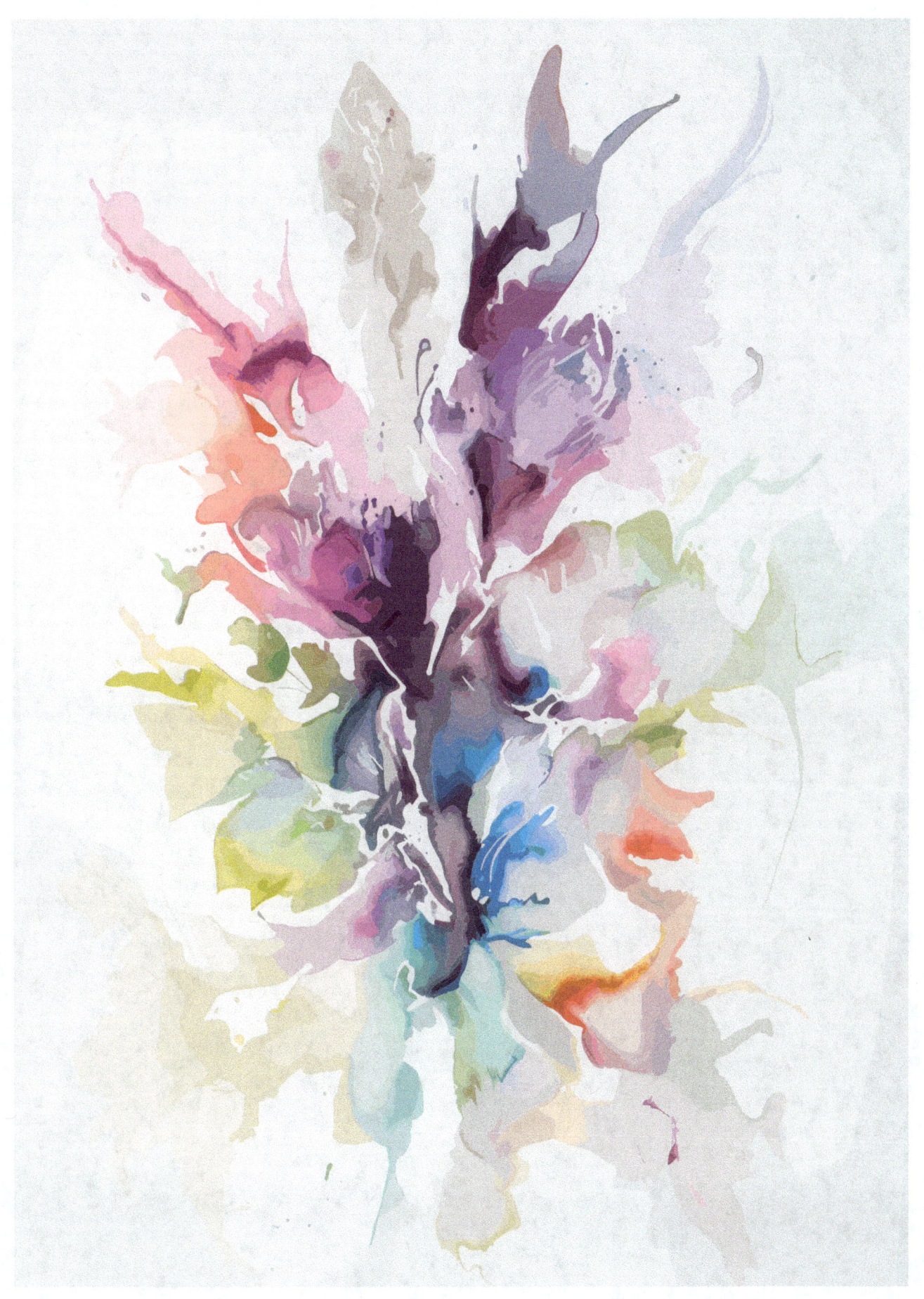

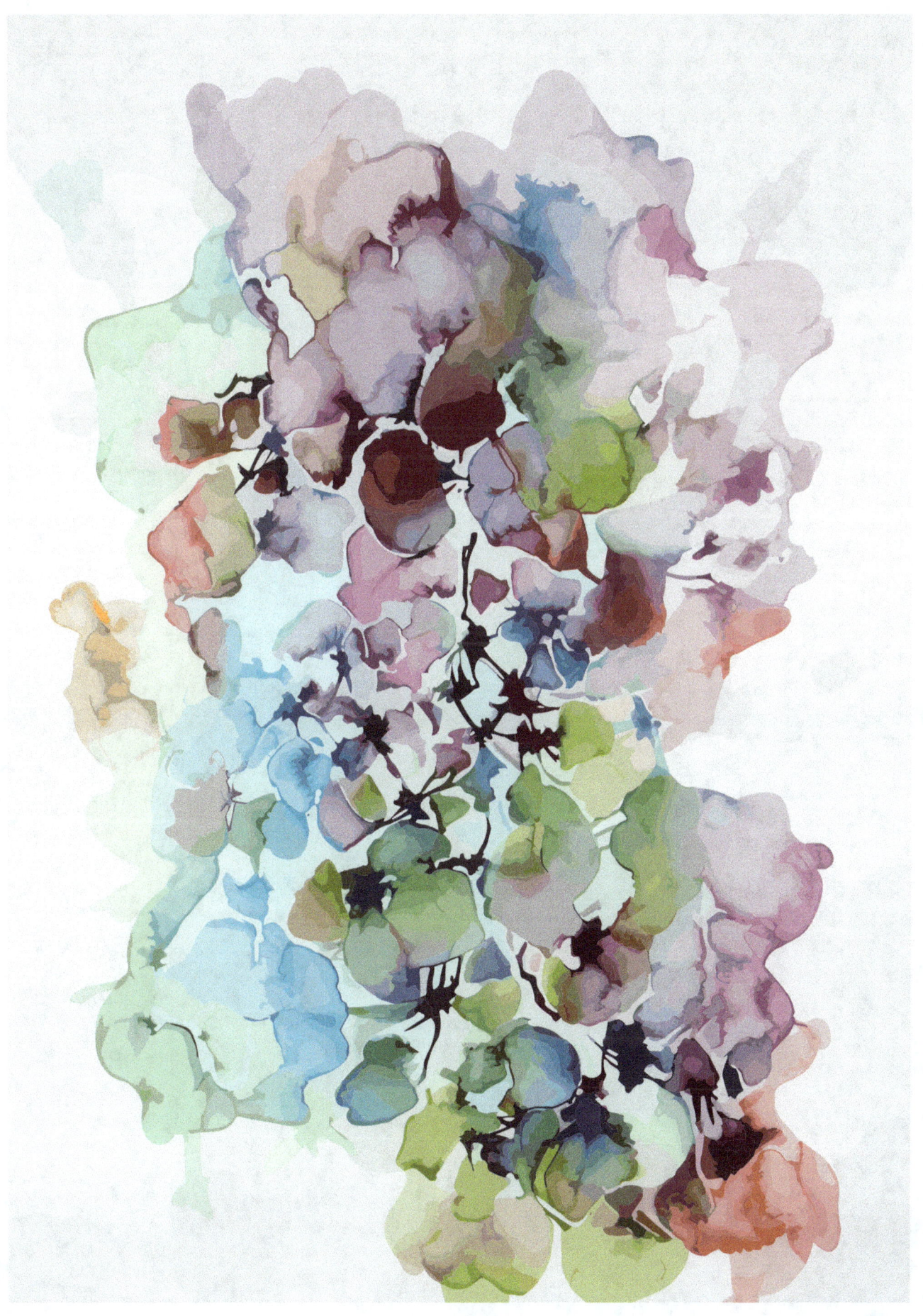

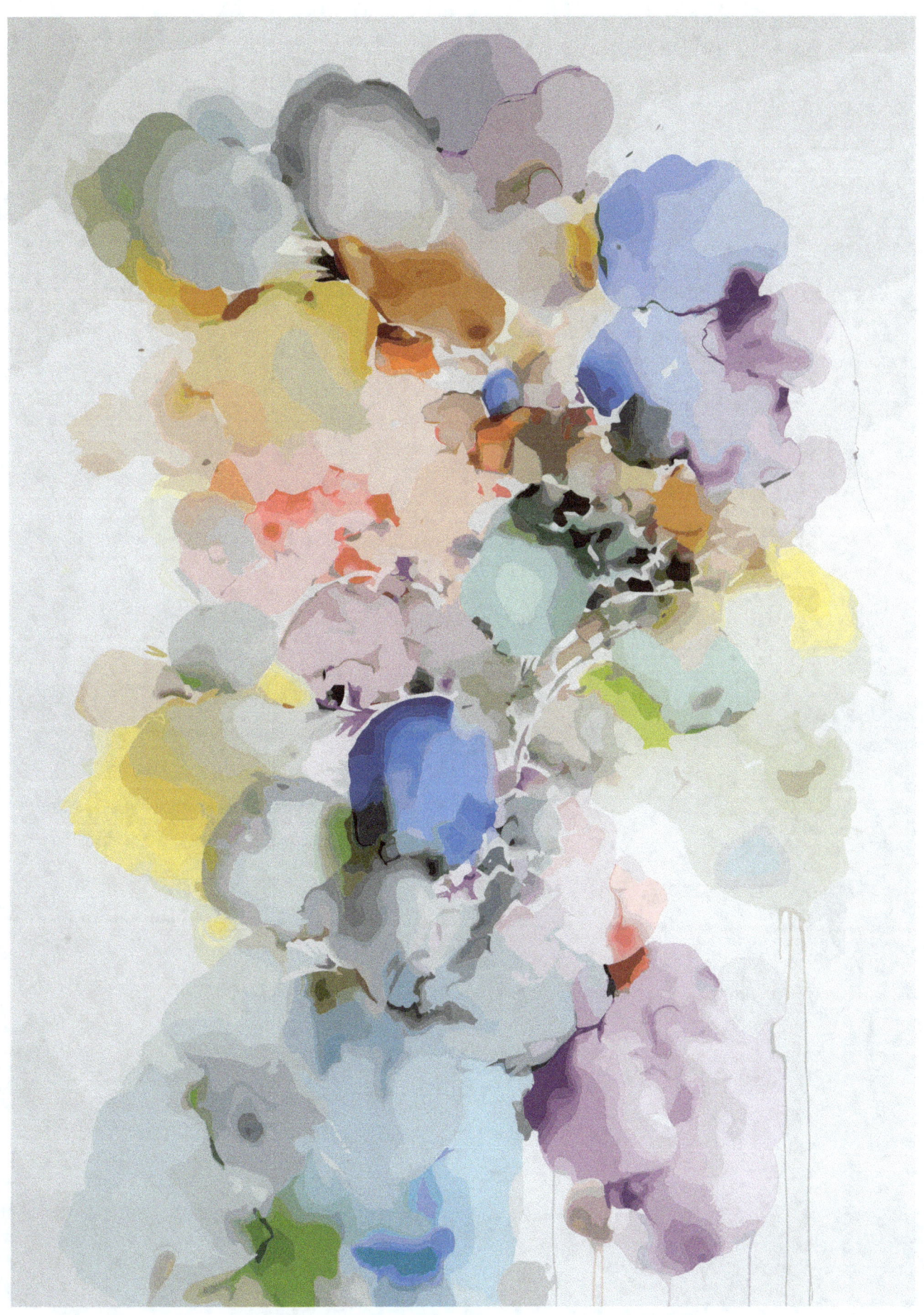

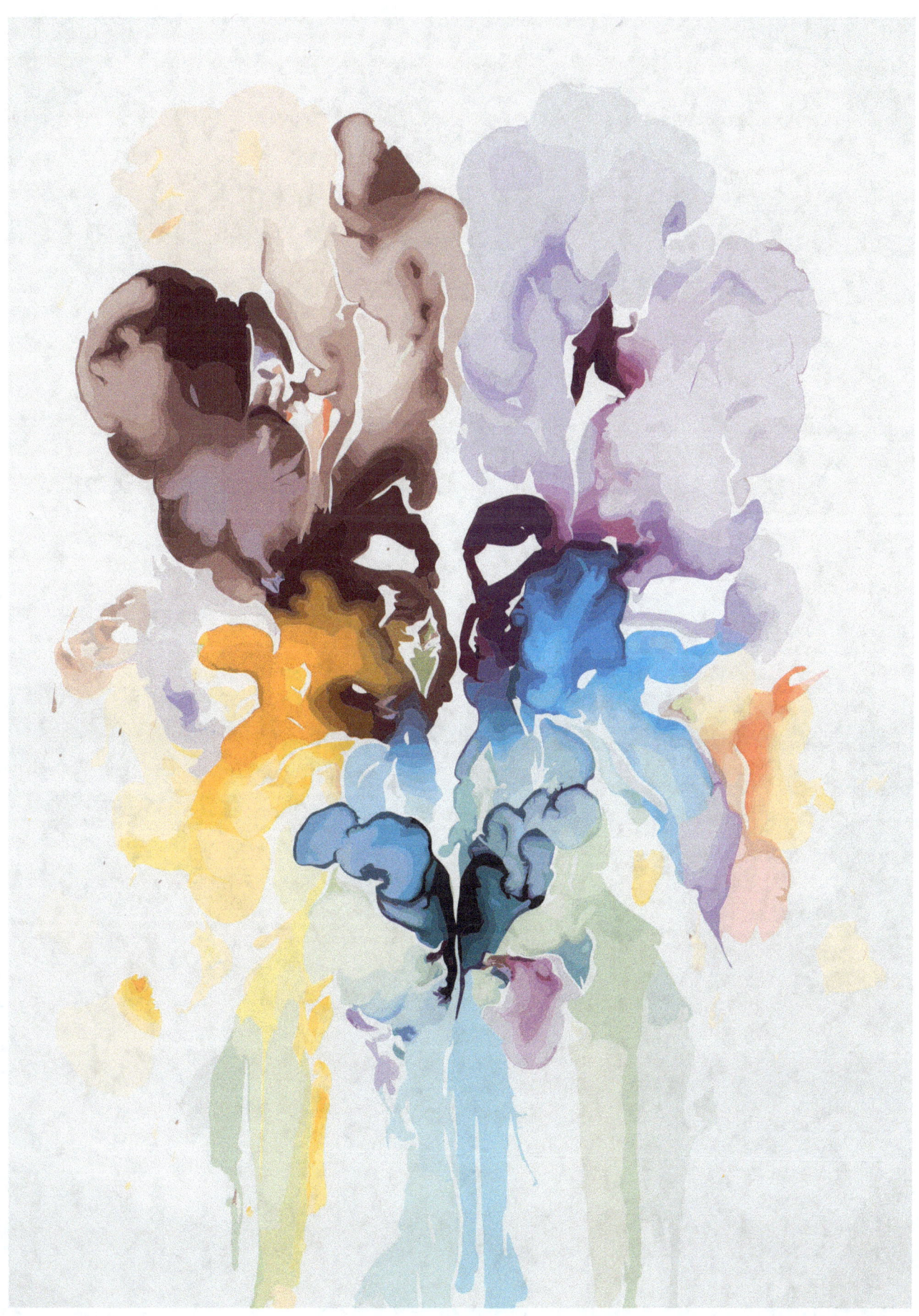

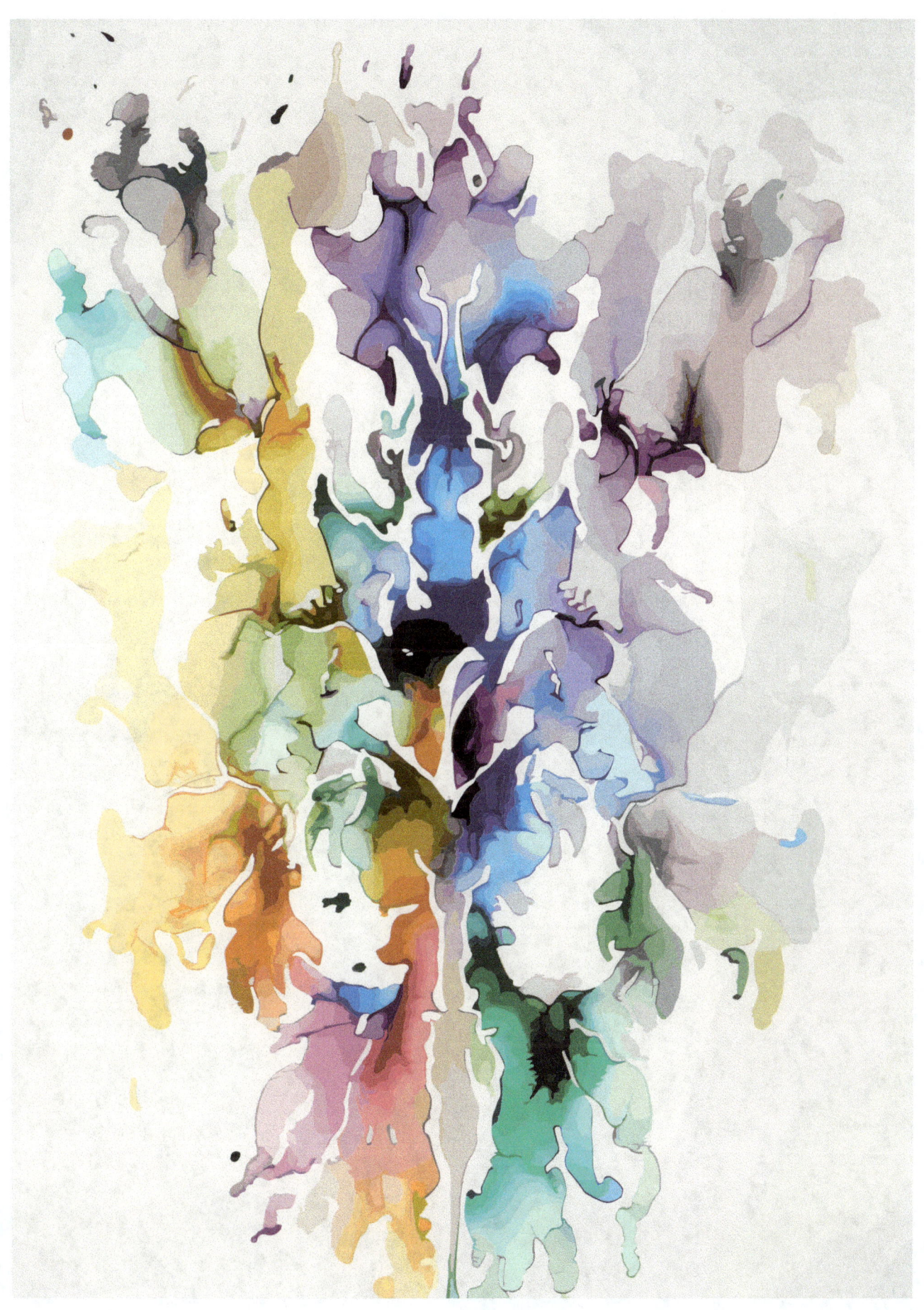

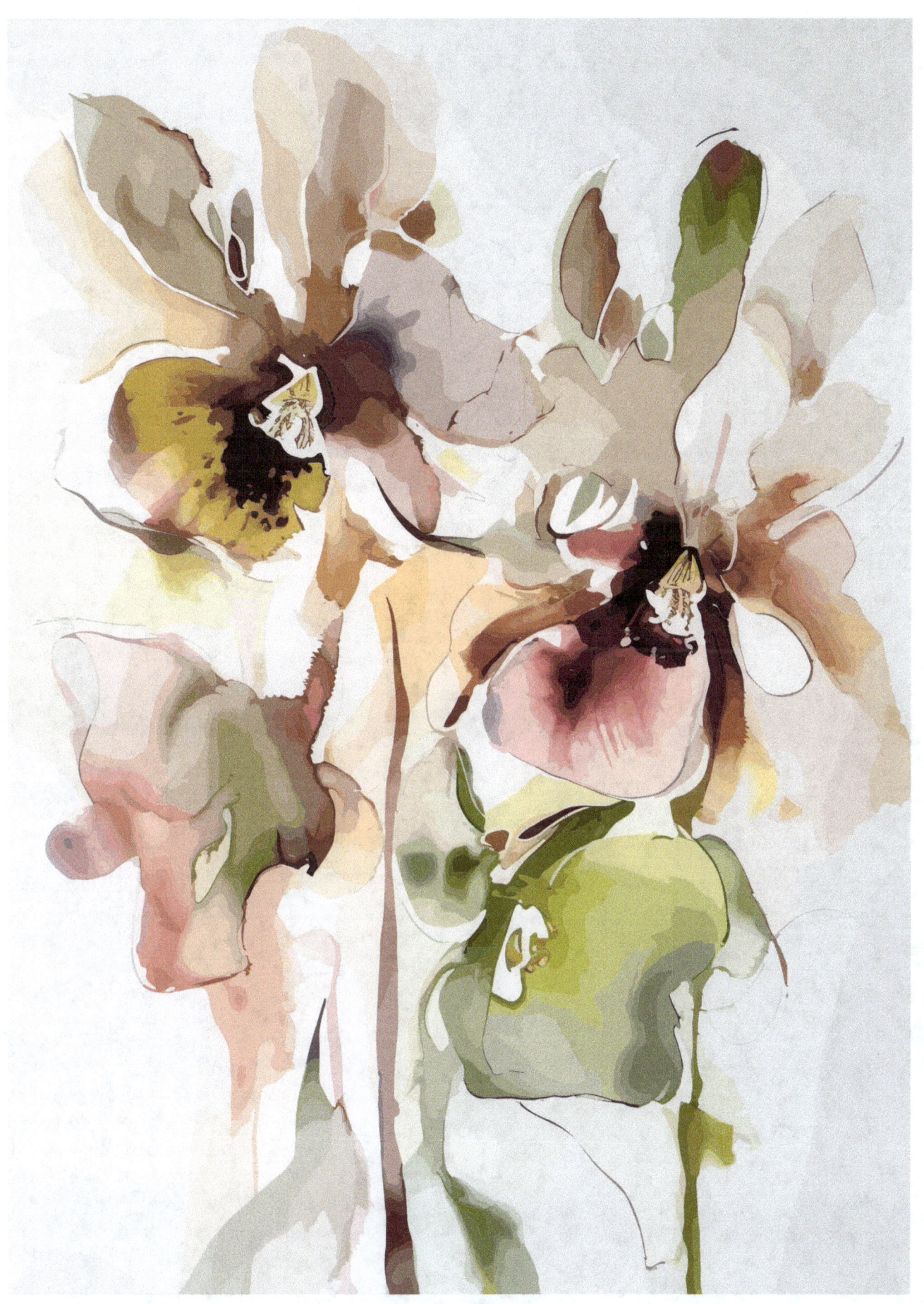

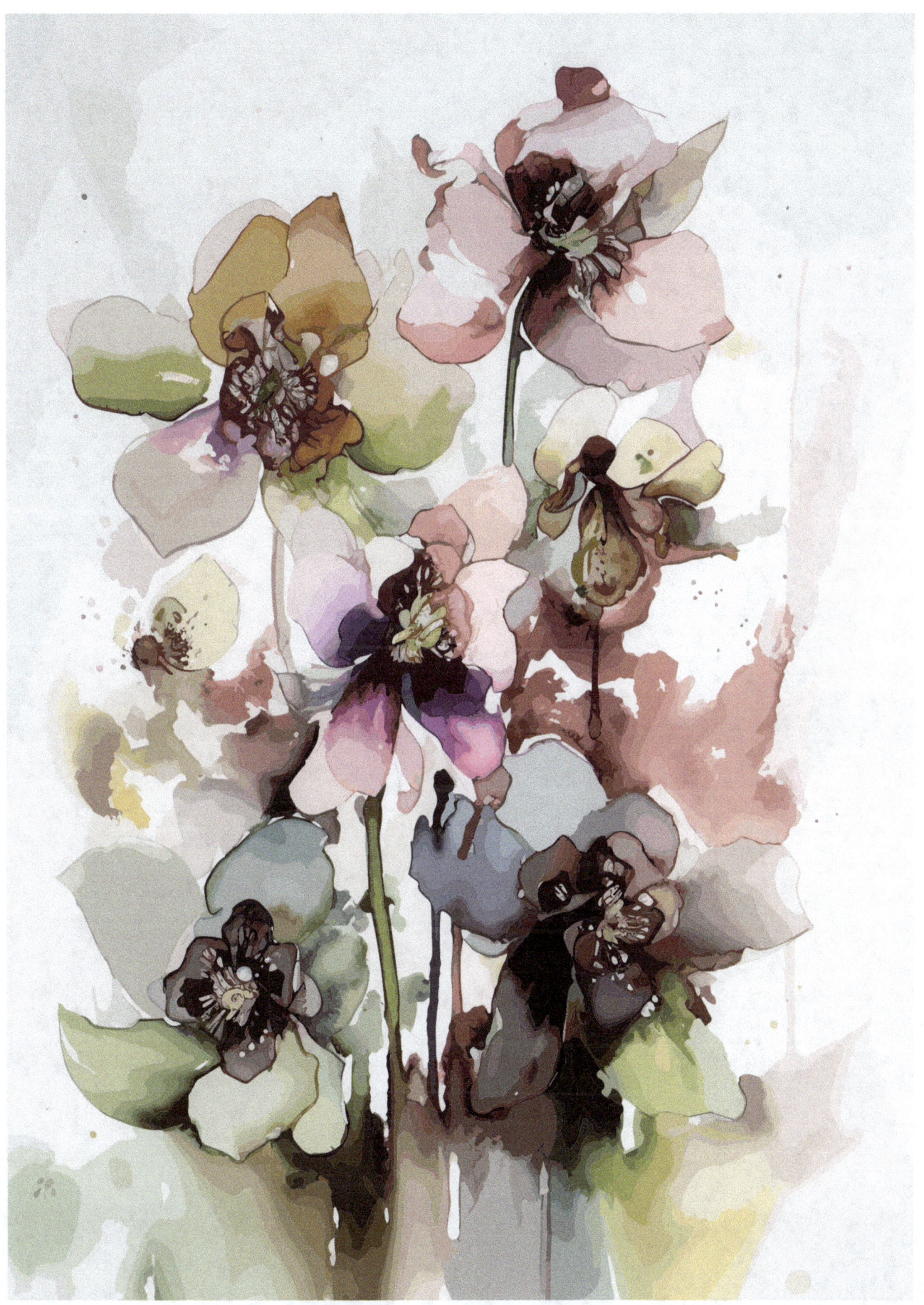

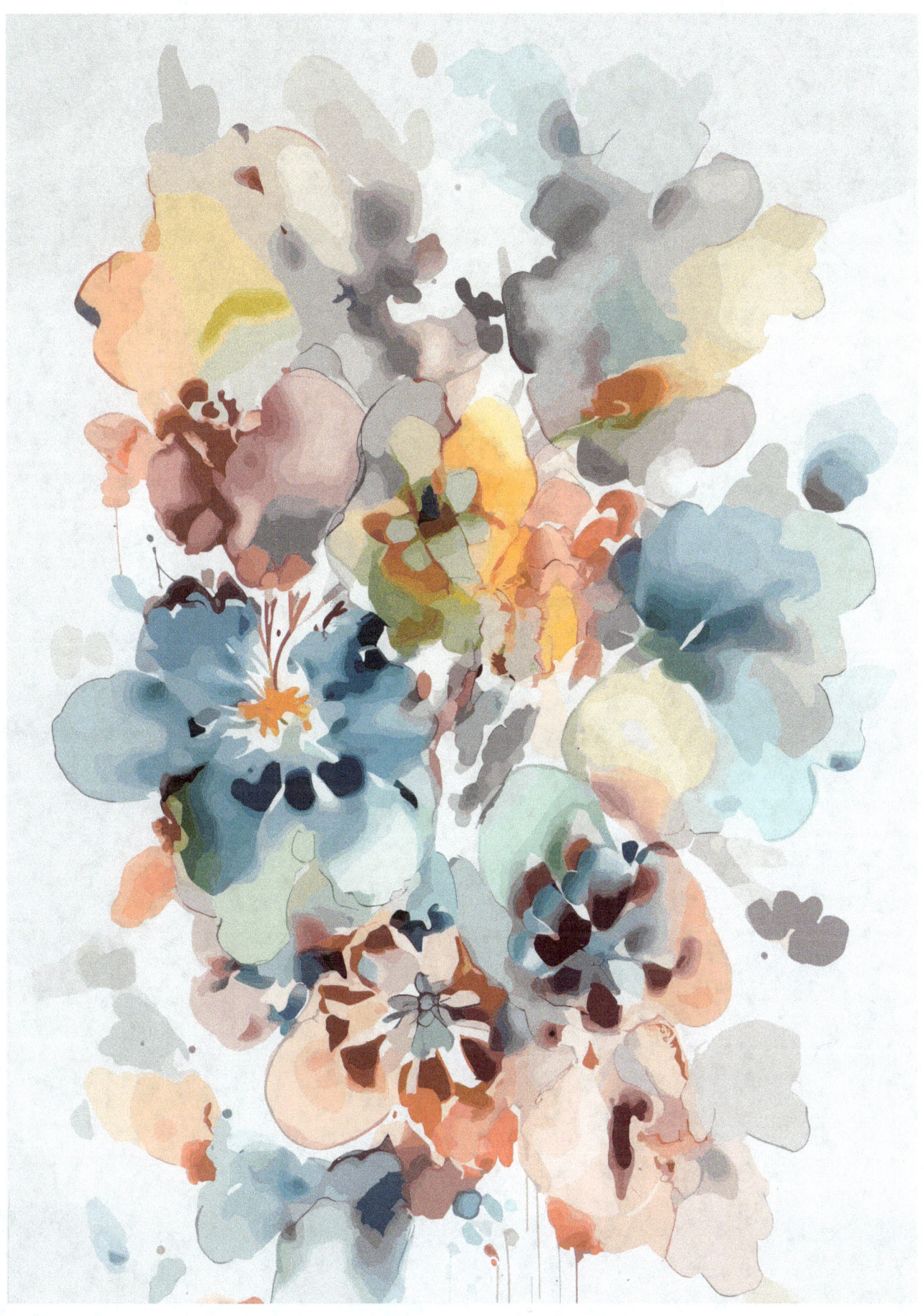

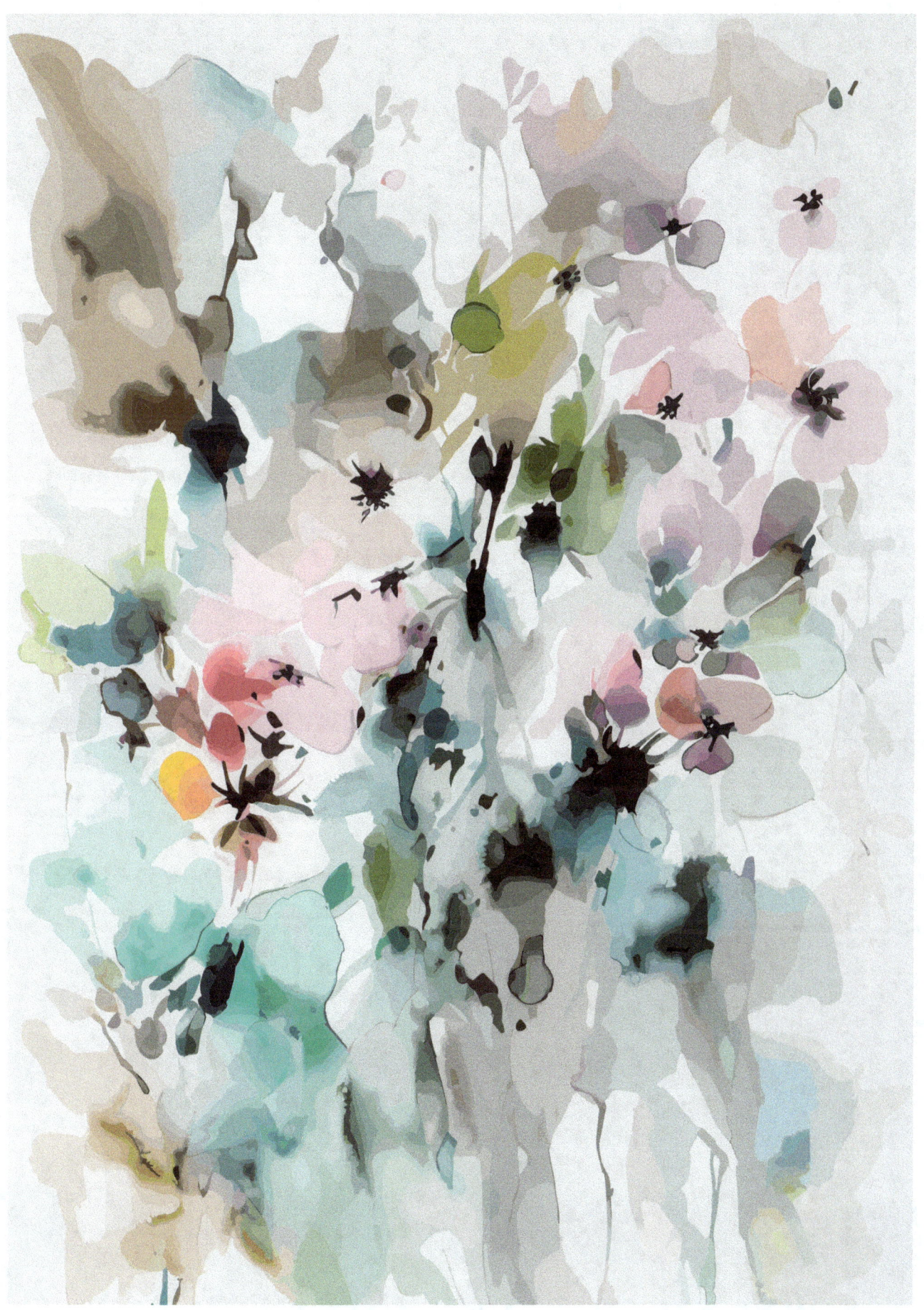

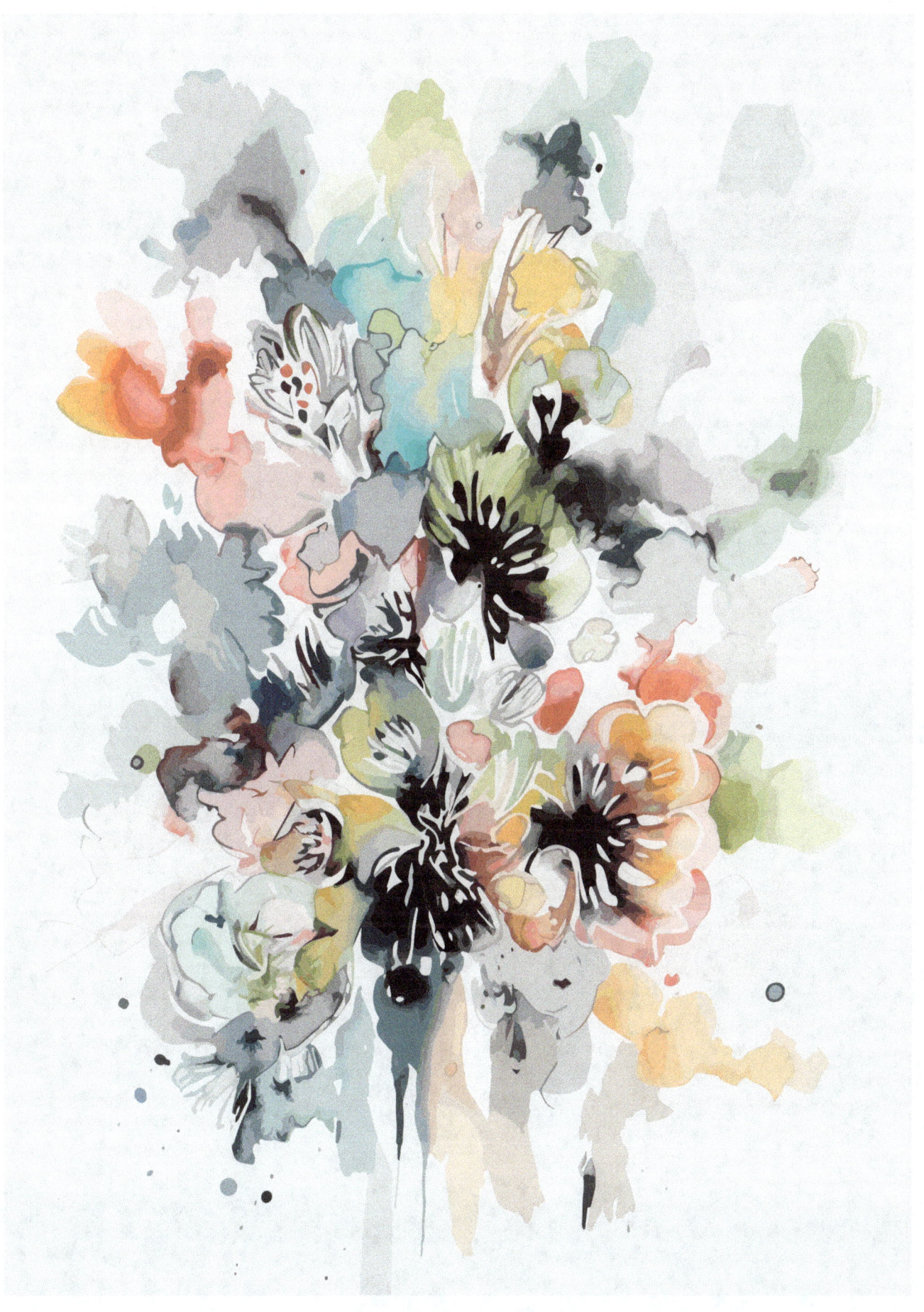

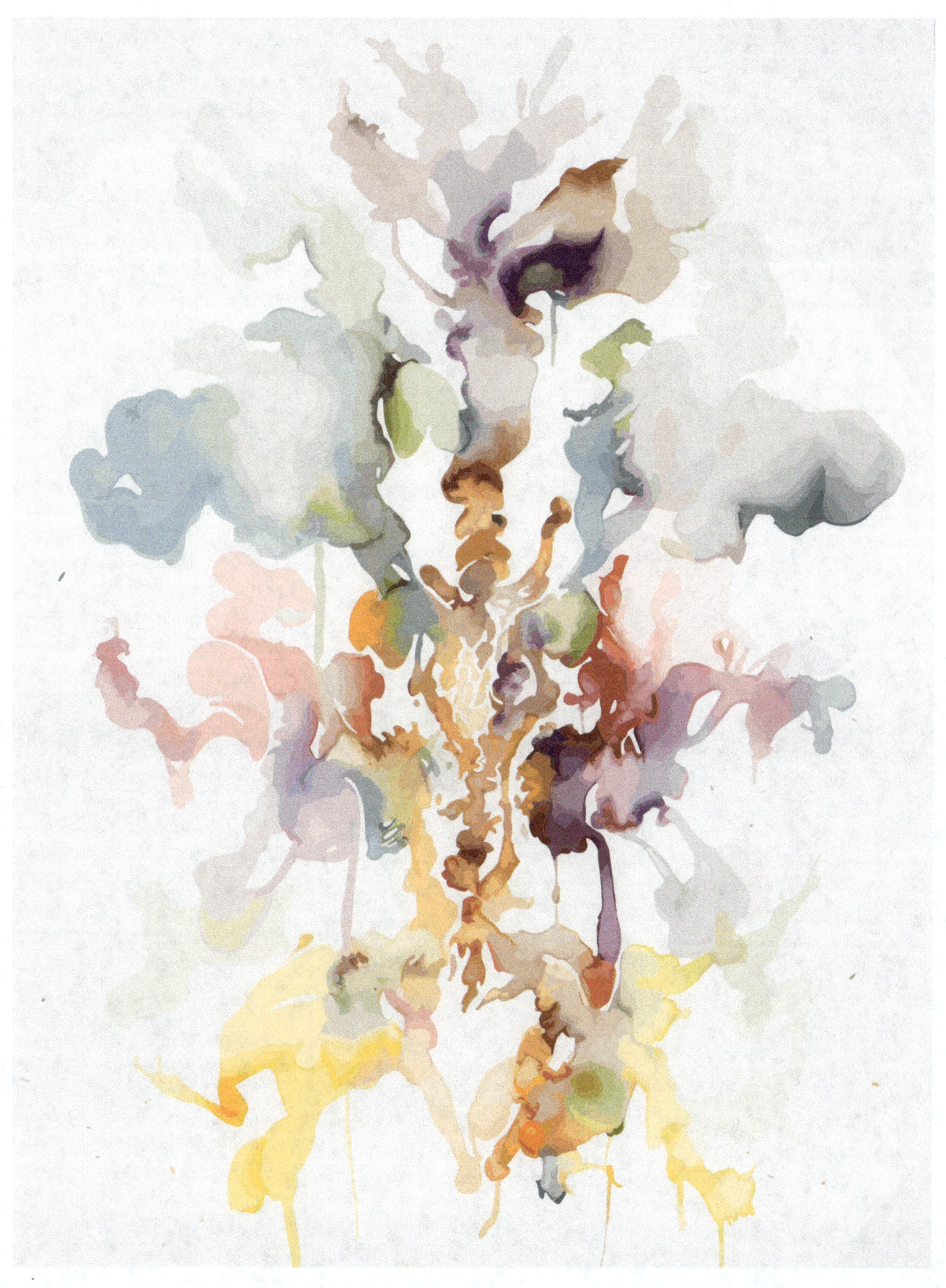

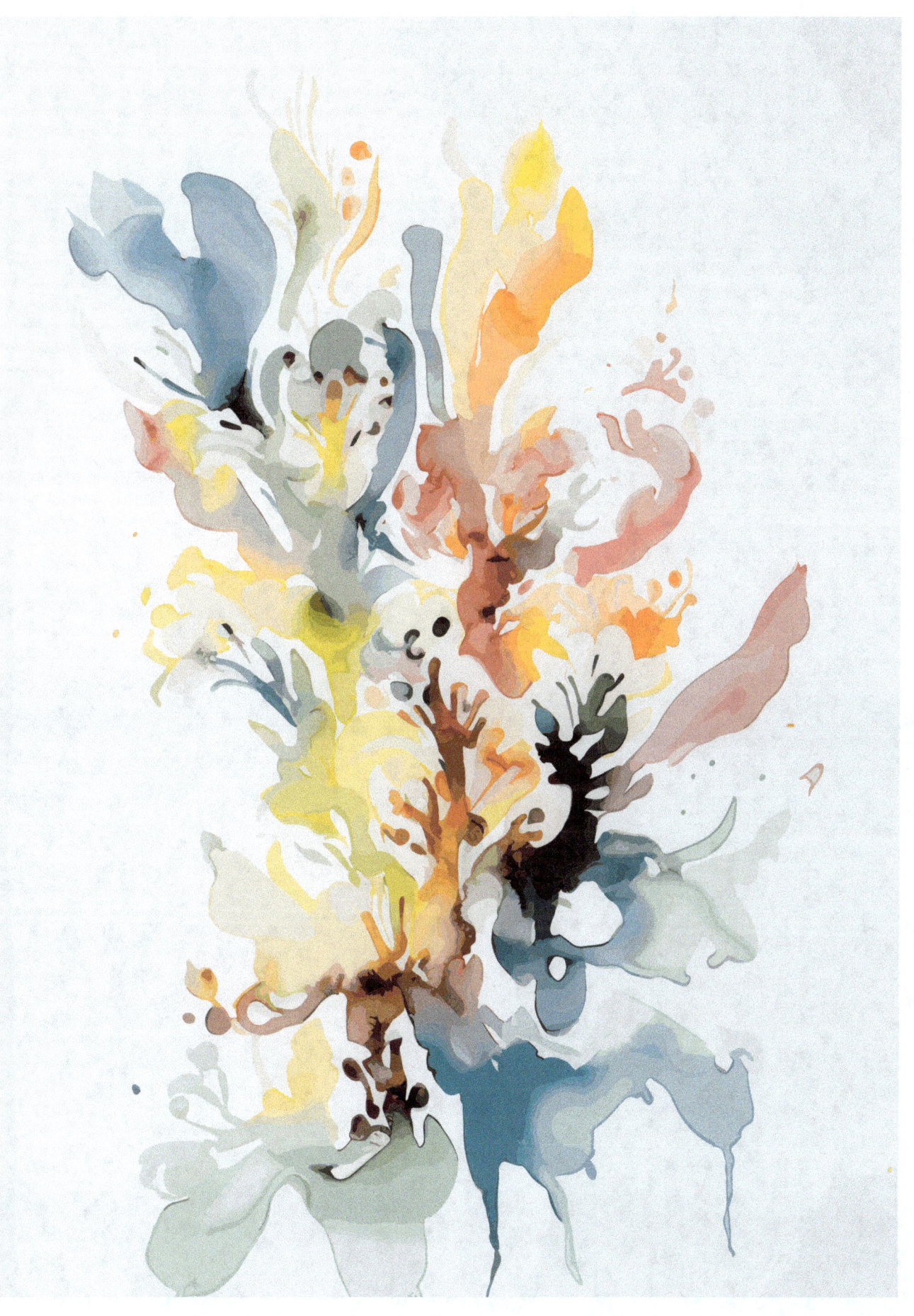

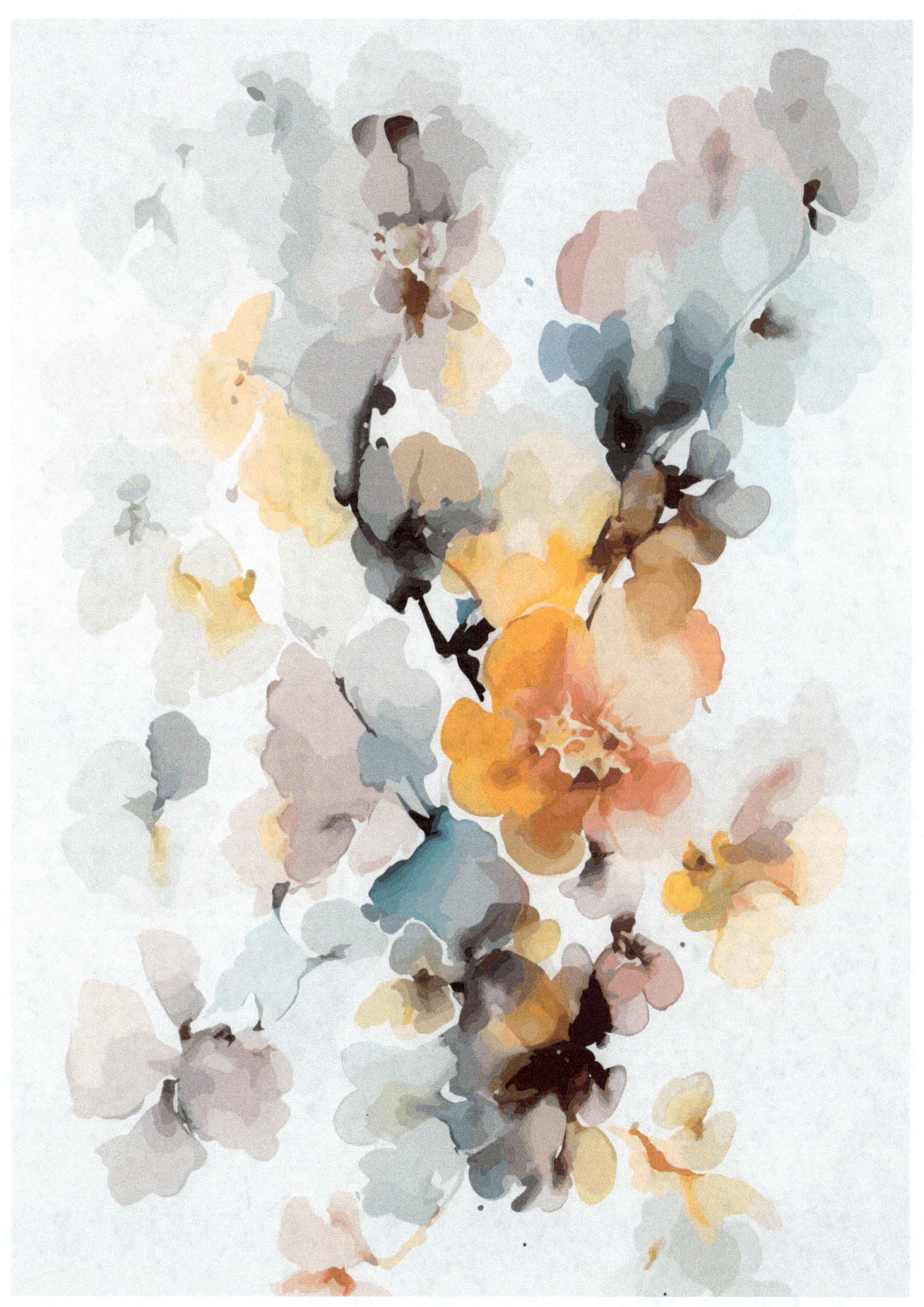

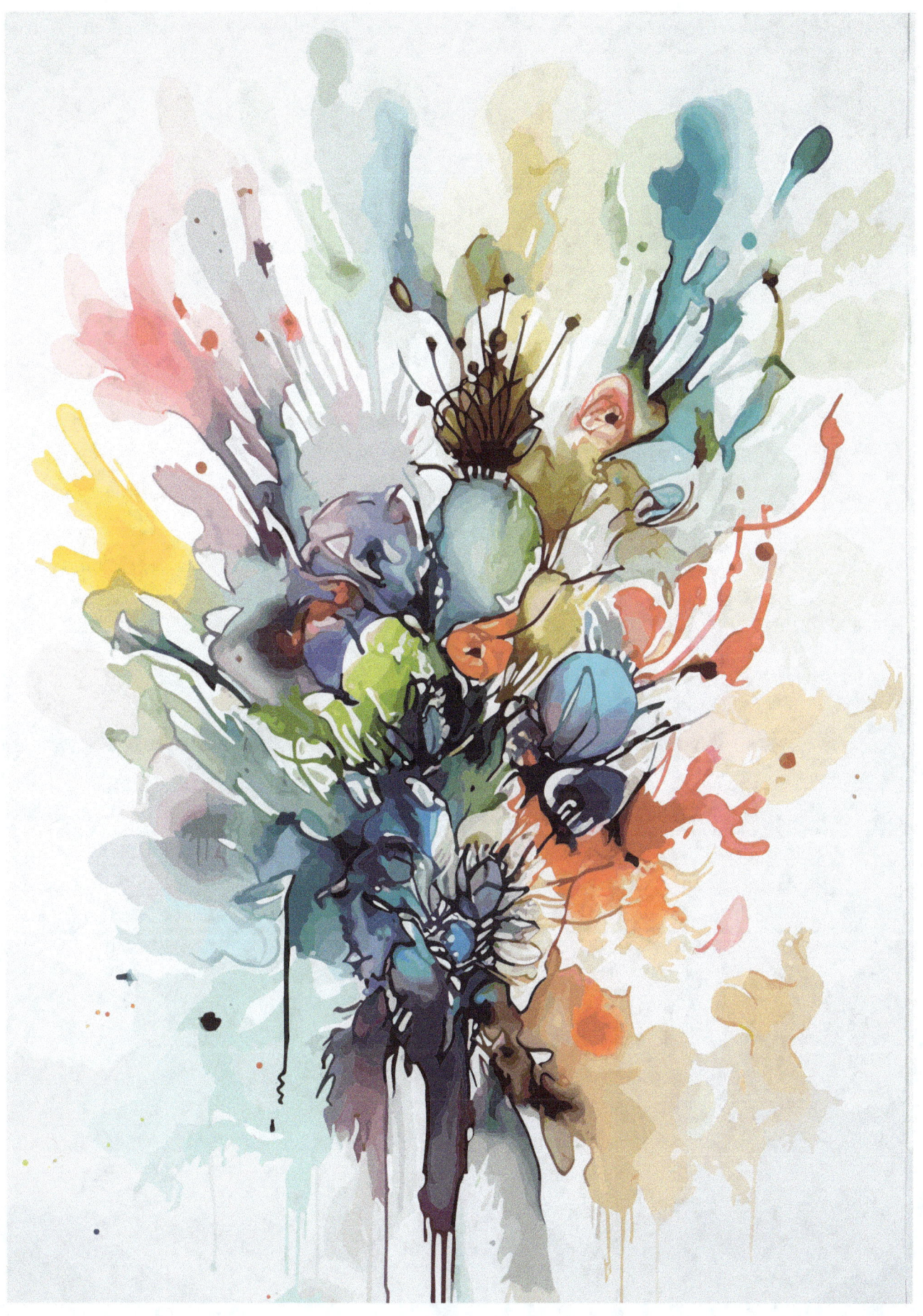

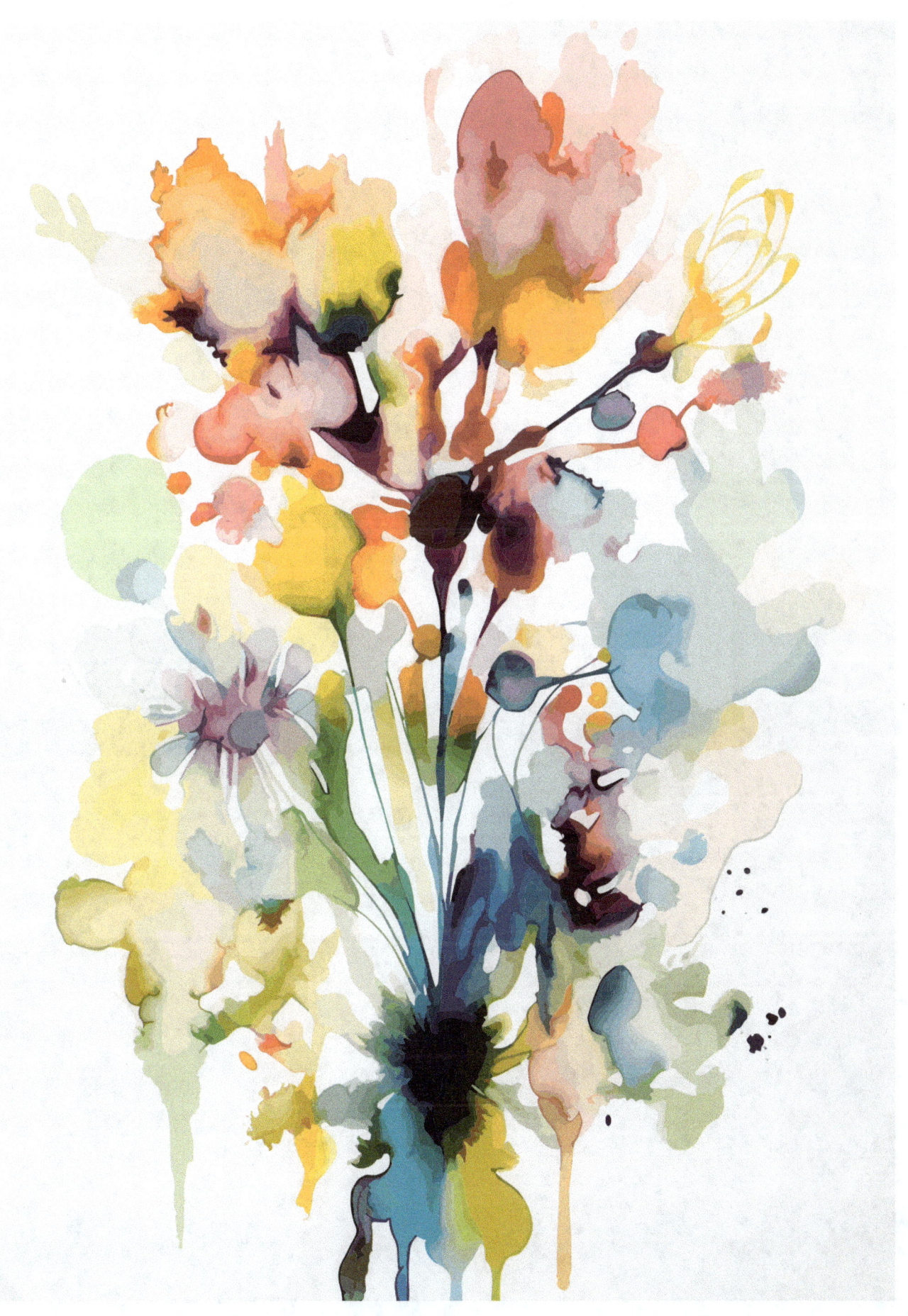

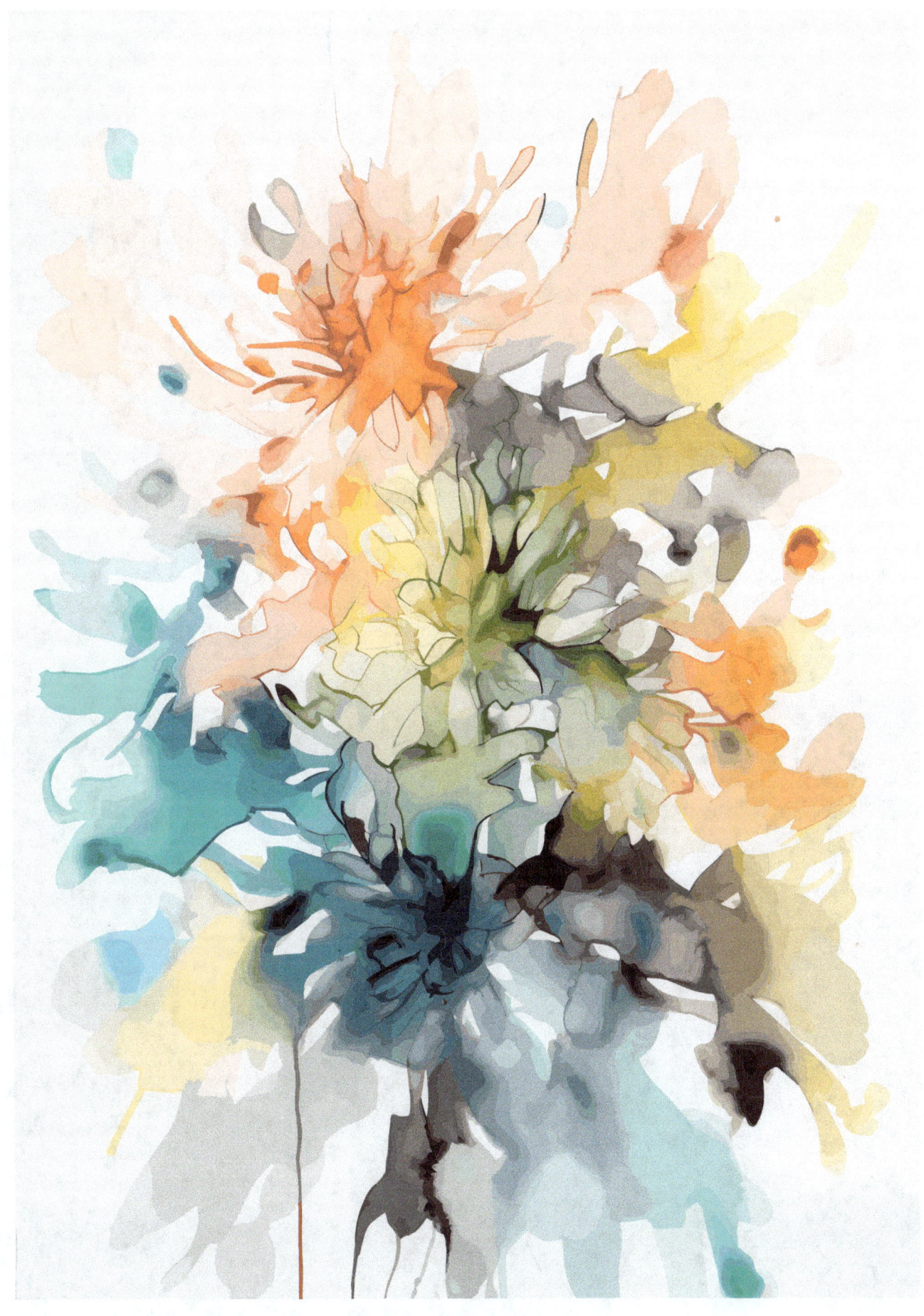

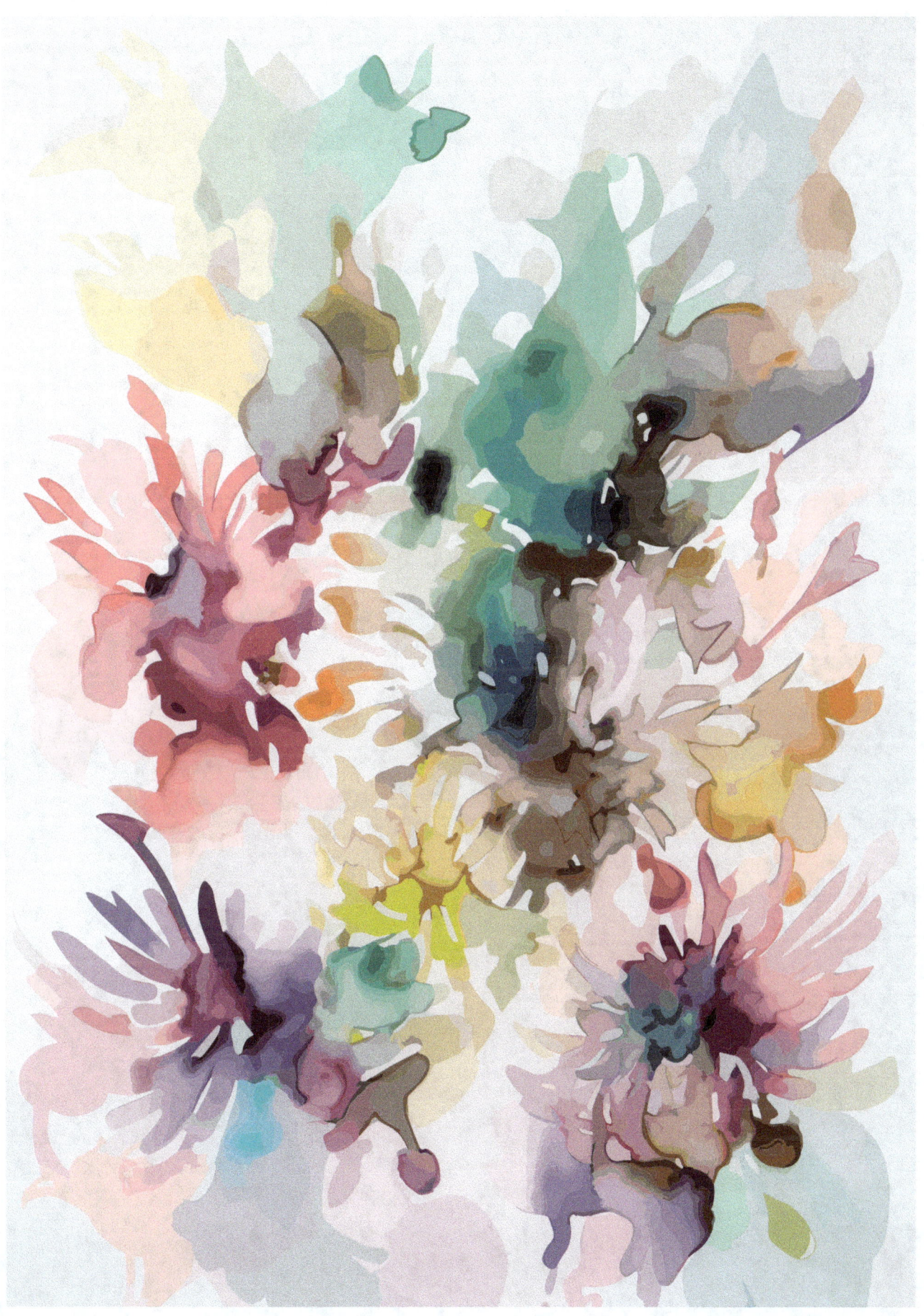

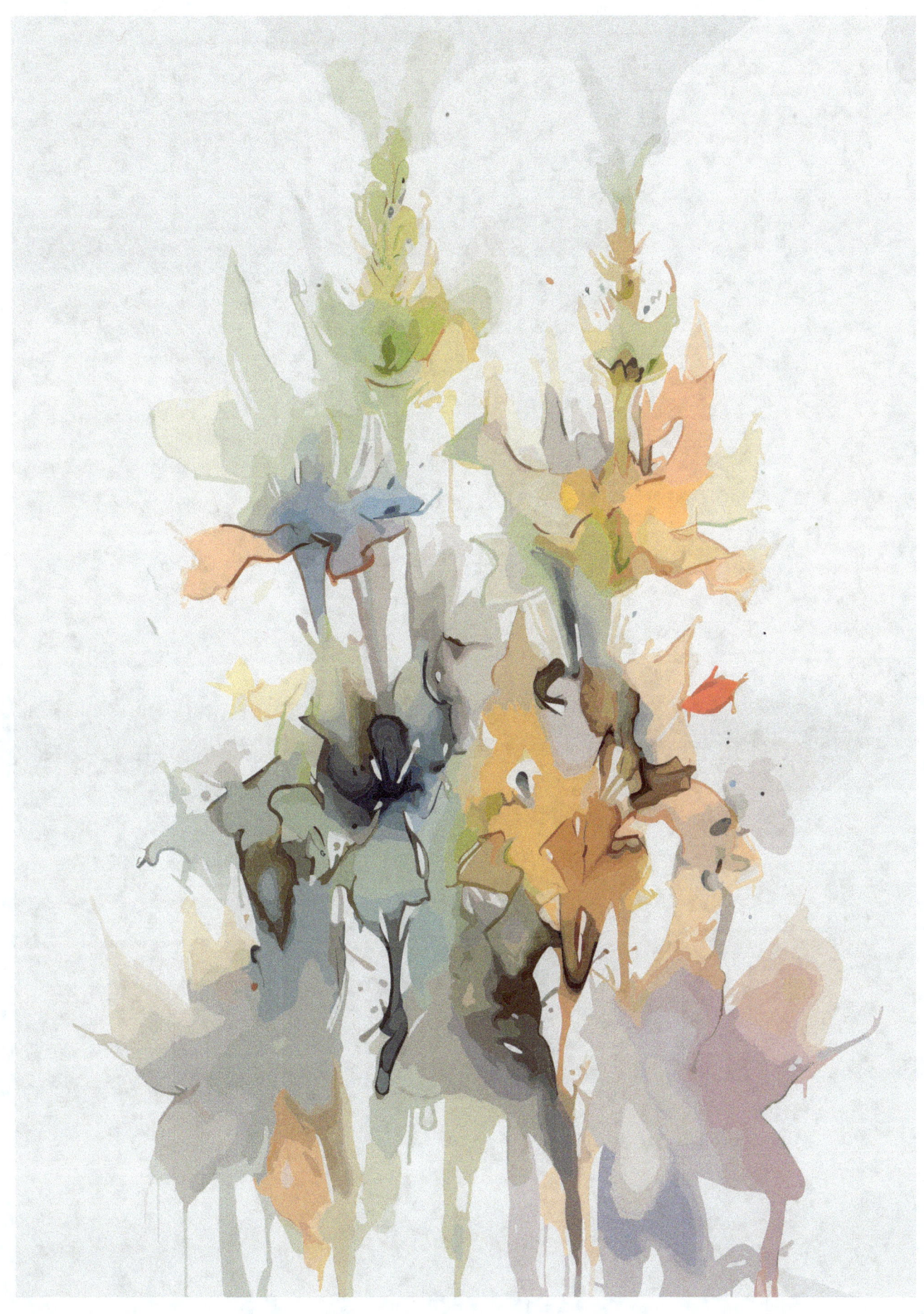

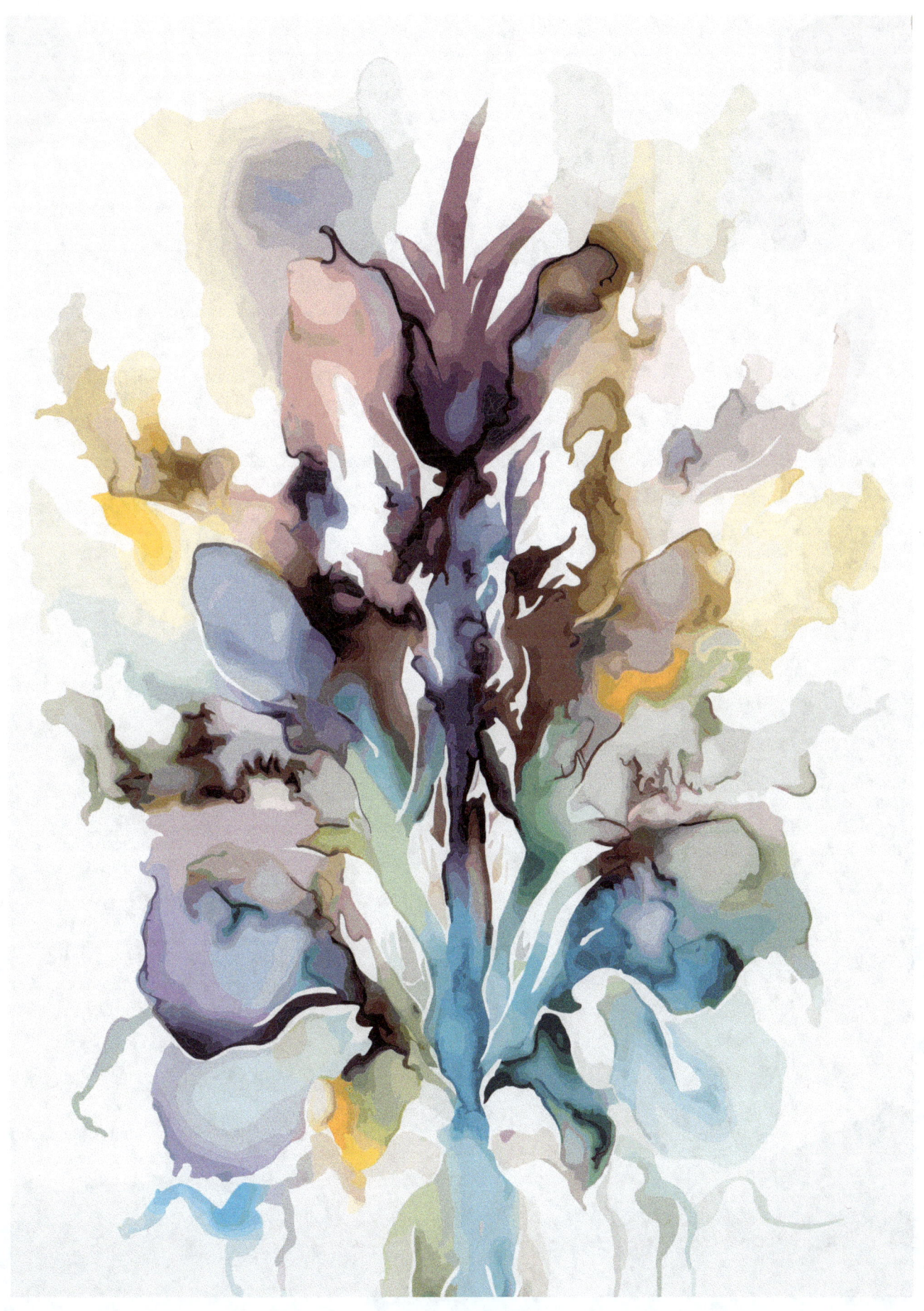

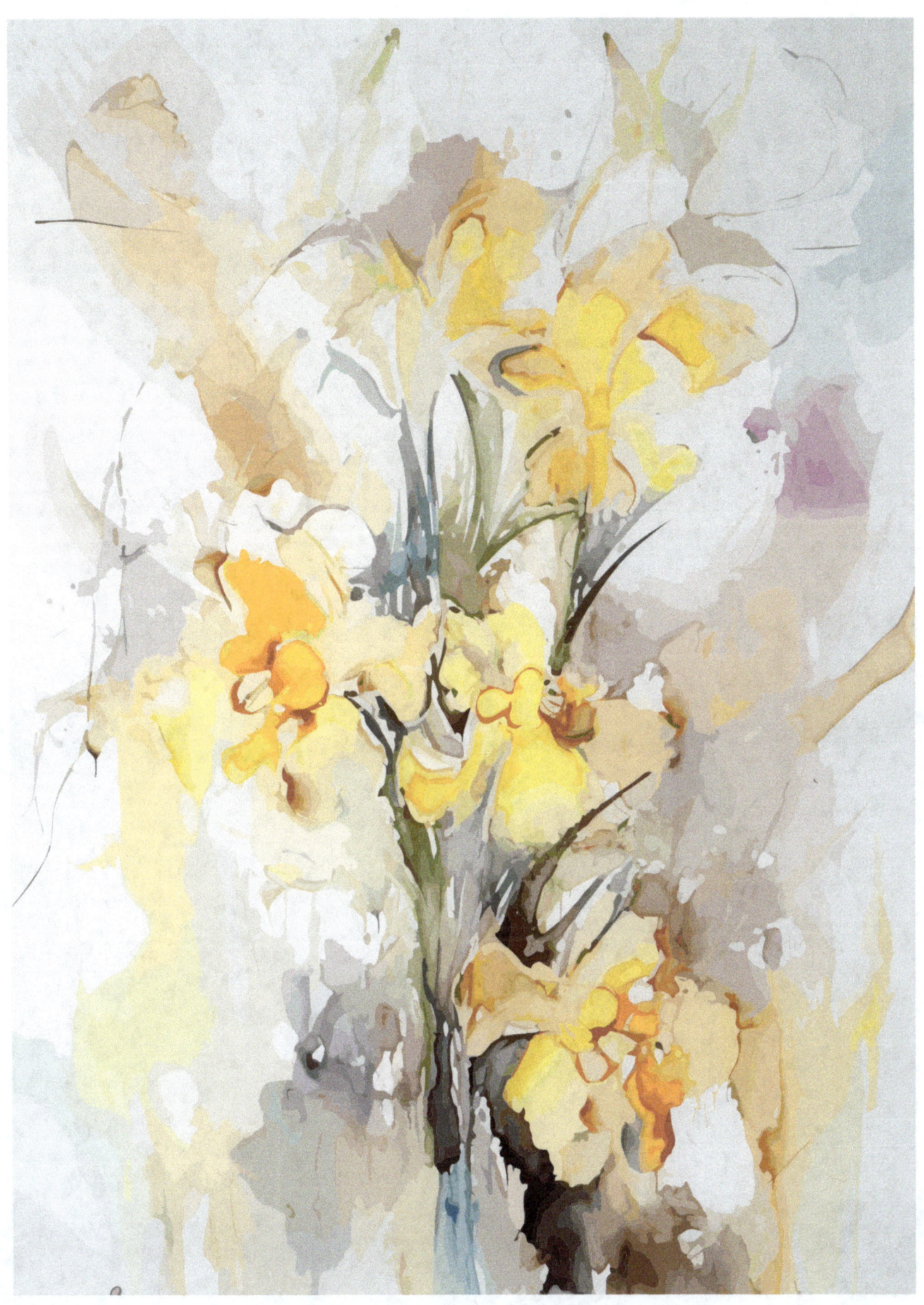

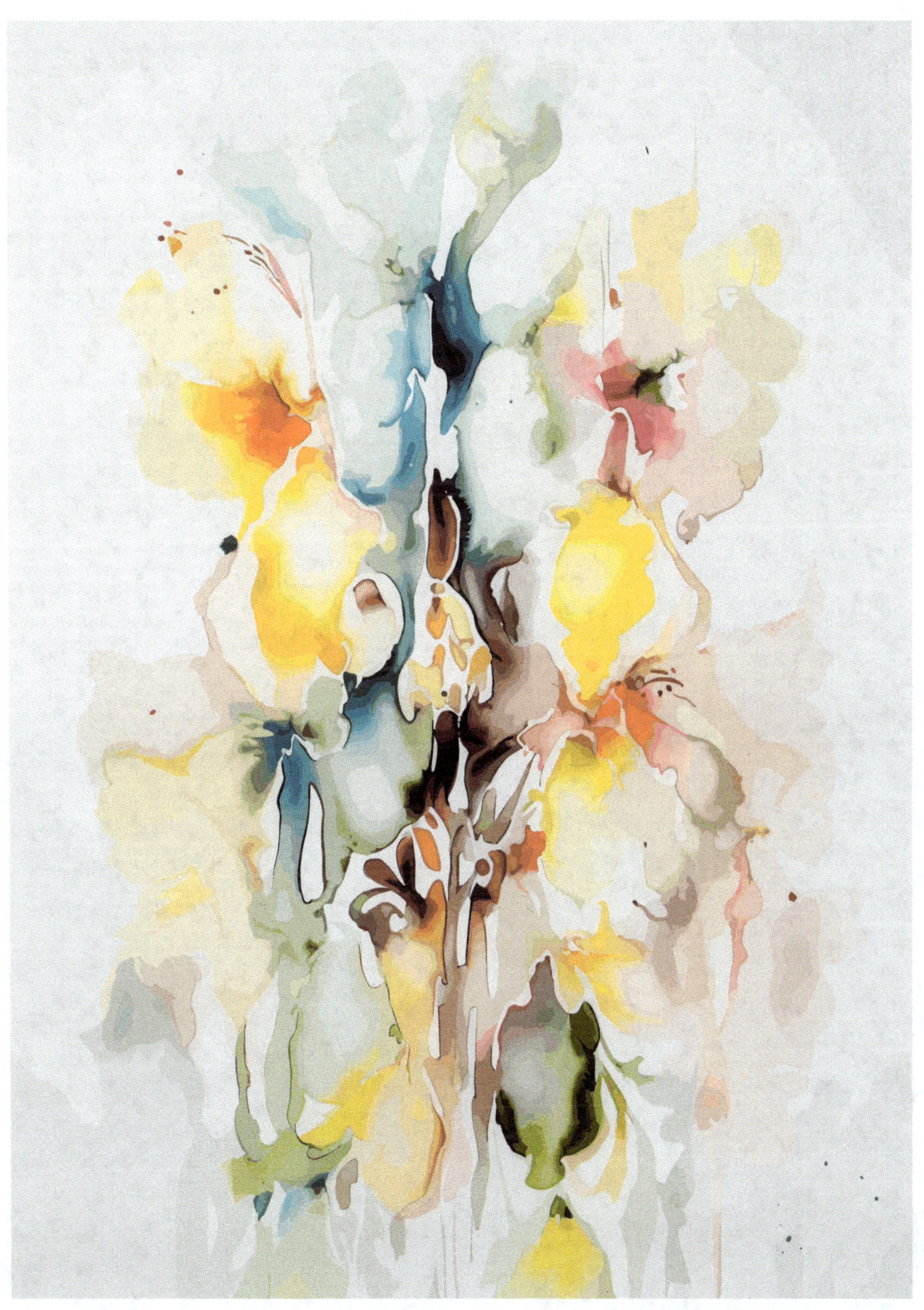

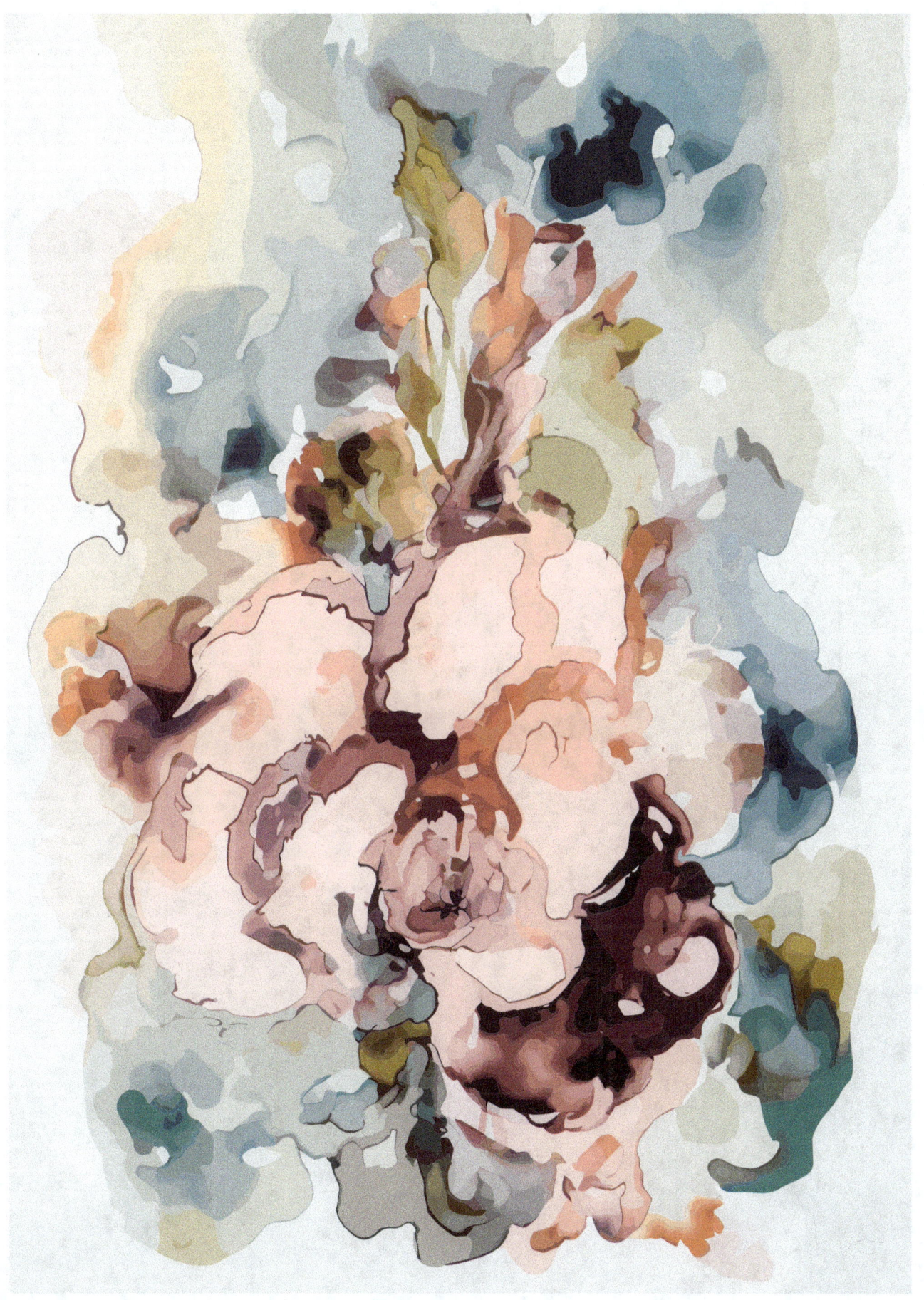

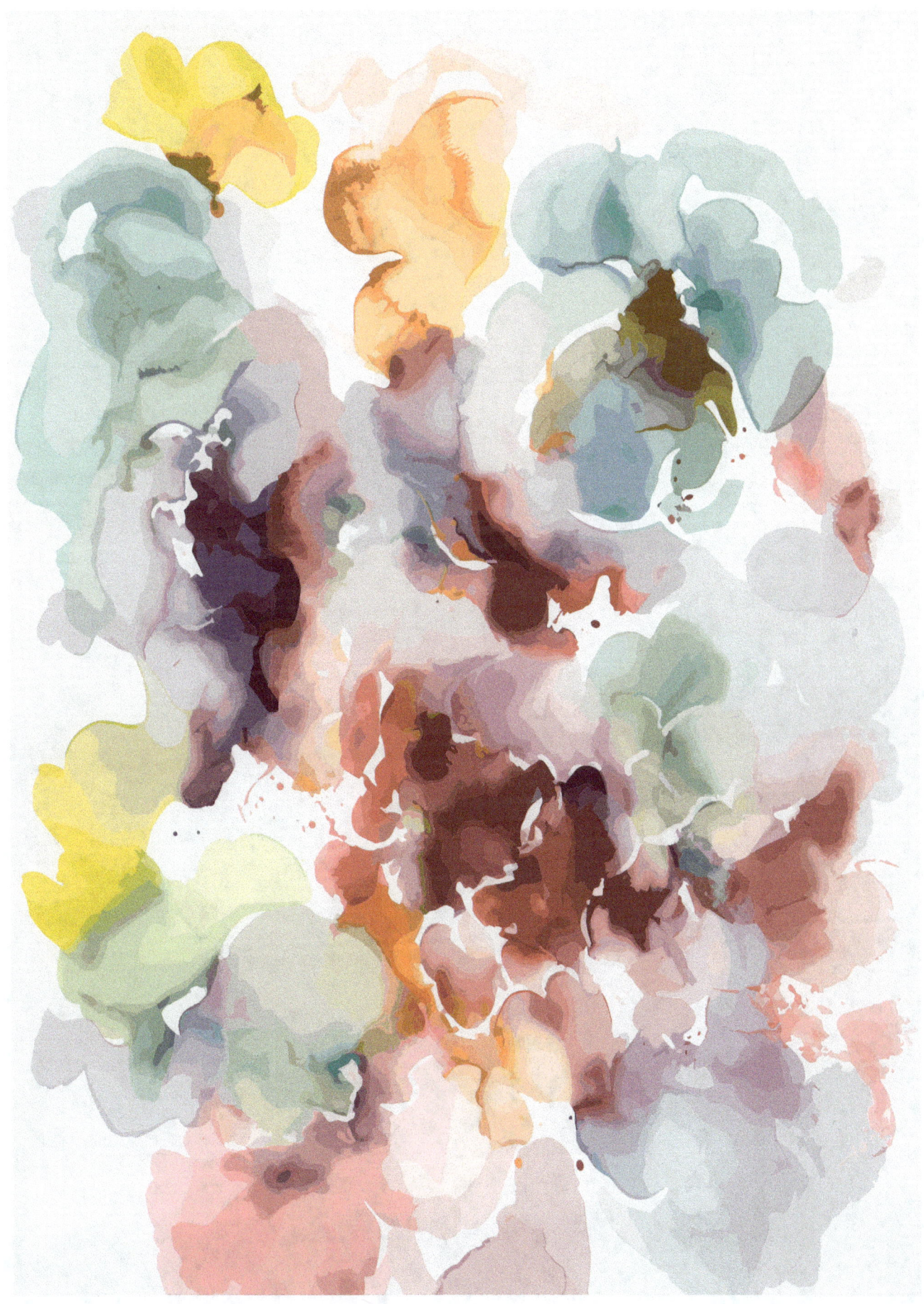

THANK YOU FOR YOUR SUPPORT
PLEASE LEAVE A REVIEW
ON AMAZON

YOUR FEEDBACK IS APPRECIATED

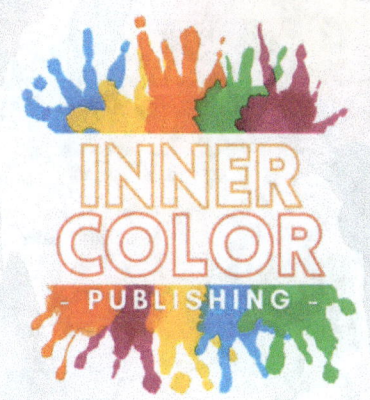